State of North Carolina Extradition Manual

Third Edition, 2013

Robert L. Farb
with Connie Eason,
former Extradition Secretary

Pat McCrory, Governor
Angie West, Extradition Secretary

UNC
SCHOOL OF
GOVERNMENT

The School of Government at the University of North Carolina at Chapel Hill works to improve the lives of North Carolinians by engaging in practical scholarship that helps public officials and citizens understand and improve state and local government. Established in 1931 as the Institute of Government, the School provides educational, advisory, and research services for state and local governments. The School of Government is also home to a nationally ranked graduate program in public administration and specialized centers focused on information technology and environmental finance.

As the largest university-based local government training, advisory, and research organization in the United States, the School of Government offers up to 200 courses, webinars, and specialized conferences for more than 12,000 public officials each year. In addition, faculty members annually publish approximately 50 books, manuals, reports, articles, bulletins, and other print and online content related to state and local government. Each day that the General Assembly is in session, the School produces the *Daily Bulletin Online*, which reports on the day's activities for members of the legislature and others who need to follow the course of legislation.

The Master of Public Administration Program is offered in two formats. The full-time, two-year residential program serves up to 60 students annually. In 2013 the School launched MPA@UNC, an online format designed for working professionals and others seeking flexibility while advancing their careers in public service. The School's MPA program consistently ranks among the best public administration graduate programs in the country, particularly in city management. With courses ranging from public policy analysis to ethics and management, the program educates leaders for local, state, and federal governments and nonprofit organizations.

Operating support for the School of Government's programs and activities comes from many sources, including state appropriations, local government membership dues, private contributions, publication sales, course fees, and service contracts. Visit www.sog.unc.edu or call 919.966.5381 for more information on the School's courses, publications, programs, and services.

Michael R. Smith, DEAN
Thomas H. Thornburg, SENIOR ASSOCIATE DEAN
Frayda S. Bluestein, ASSOCIATE DEAN FOR FACULTY DEVELOPMENT
L. Ellen Bradley, ASSOCIATE DEAN FOR PROGRAMS AND MARKETING
Todd A. Nicolet, ASSOCIATE DEAN FOR OPERATIONS
Ann Cary Simpson, ASSOCIATE DEAN FOR DEVELOPMENT
Bradley G. Volk, ASSOCIATE DEAN FOR ADMINISTRATION

FACULTY

Whitney Afonso	Richard D. Ducker	Christopher B. McLaughlin	Karl W. Smith
Trey Allen	Joseph S. Ferrell	Laurie L. Mesibov	Meredith Smith
Gregory S. Allison	Alyson A. Grine	Kara A. Millonzi	Carl W. Stenberg III
David N. Ammons	Norma Houston	Jill D. Moore	John B. Stephens
Ann M. Anderson	Cheryl Daniels Howell	Jonathan Q. Morgan	Charles Szypszak
A. Fleming Bell, II	Jeffrey A. Hughes	Ricardo S. Morse	Shannon H. Tufts
Maureen M. Berner	Willow S. Jacobson	C. Tyler Mulligan	Vaughn Upshaw
Mark F. Botts	Robert P. Joyce	David W. Owens	Aimee N. Wall
Michael Crowell	Kenneth L. Joyner	LaToya B. Powell	Jeffrey B. Welty
Sara DePasquale	Diane M. Juffras	William C. Rivenbark	Richard B. Whisnant
Leisha DeHart-Davis	Dona G. Lewandowski	Dale J. Roenigk	
Shea Riggsbee Denning	Adam Lovelady	John Rubin	
James C. Drennan	James M. Markham	Jessica Smith	

Author Acknowledgment

Robert L. Farb is a retired professor of public law and government, with a long history at the School of Government. He continues as an adjunct professor of public law and government to work on occasional special projects in criminal law and procedure, a field in which he is widely published.

Connie Eason, who assisted in the preparation of this manual, retired as extradition secretary for North Carolina on February 27, 2015. Angie West replaced her.

Angie West
Extradition Secretary
State of North Carolina
Department of Justice
Post Office Box 629
Raleigh, North Carolina 27602
Phone: (919) 716-6500
FAX: (919) 716-6760
email: anwest@ncdoj.gov

Office of the Governor
Administration Building
116 West Jones Street
MSC-20301
Raleigh, NC 27699-0301
Phone: (919) 814-2000
FAX: (919) 733-2100

Contents

Introduction

Extradition is the procedure by which a person who committed a crime in one state or was convicted and while awaiting sentencing fled to another state (or escaped from prison or violated probation, parole, or post-release supervision) is returned to the first state. This manual seeks to give the reader a broad overview of the extradition process. For those officials who play a limited role, such as the arresting officer or the magistrate, this general description should help them understand how their actions fit into the overall process. Later sections provide more specific instructions for the different stages in the extradition process. In addition, the manual discusses other statutes and issues that do not directly involve extradition but are related to it, such as the Interstate Agreement on Detainers.

Overview

Article IV, Section 2 of the United States Constitution and federal statutory law (18 U.S.C. § 3182) require that a person charged with treason, felony, or other crime who flees from justice and is found in another state shall, on demand of the governor of the state from which the person fled, be delivered for return to the state having jurisdiction over the crime. More detailed procedures are set out in the Uniform Criminal Extradition Act, which North Carolina and most other states as well as U.S. territories have adopted. While these state statutes are similar to the uniform act, extradition practice varies somewhat from state to state. For example, many states will not extradite for misdemeanors. The extradition secretary knows the peculiar requirements of other states and tries to review all documents to be certain they will satisfy the recipient state.

Returning Fugitive Found in North Carolina to Another State

To begin, consider the case of a person who committed a serious crime—say, armed robbery—in another state, Ohio, and then fled to North Carolina. Probably that person has already been formally charged in Ohio, either by indictment or by the issuance of an arrest warrant there. When the person's presence in North Carolina is discovered, he or she may be arrested by a North Carolina officer, either with or without an arrest warrant from a North Carolina magistrate or judge. (*Note:* Section 15A-733 of the North Carolina General Statutes (hereafter G.S.) limits the issuance of a fugitive warrant to a magistrate or judge. It does not authorize a clerk to do so. Because a warrant is usually issued by a magistrate instead of a judge, that term will be used throughout this manual.)

An arrest without a warrant, which is the less common practice, may be made only if the crime committed in Ohio is punishable there by more than one year's imprisonment. After arresting without a warrant, the officer must take the defendant before a North Carolina magistrate without unnecessary delay for issuance of a magistrate's order (AOC-CR-909M, available from the N.C. Court System website[1]), just as the officer would do if he or she were making an arrest for a crime committed in this state. (*Note*: G.S. 15A-734 effectively limits the issuance of a magistrate's order for a fugitive to a magistrate or judge. It does not authorize a clerk to do so. Because a magistrate's order is usually issued by a magistrate instead of a judge, that term will be used throughout this manual.) The magistrate determines whether the person is charged in Ohio with armed robbery, whether armed robbery is punishable by more than one year's imprisonment in Ohio, and whether the person fled from Ohio. The magistrate does not try to determine whether there is probable cause to believe the person committed the armed robbery, only whether the person is so charged in Ohio. If the magistrate finds that

---

1. AOC-CR-909M is available at www.nccourts.org/Forms/Documents/168.pdf.

such is the case, bail is authorized, unless the crime is punishable by either death or life imprisonment.

More likely, the officer will go to a magistrate to obtain a North Carolina arrest warrant, called a fugitive warrant (AOC-CR-910M, available from the N.C. Court System website[2]), before making the arrest. In that case, it is not necessary that the crime be punishable by more than one year's imprisonment; a warrant may be issued if the defendant has been charged with any crime in another state. Once the fugitive warrant is issued, the officer is to make the arrest and take the defendant before the magistrate without unnecessary delay for the setting of bail, just as the officer would for a North Carolina crime.

The usual basis for determining that the defendant has been charged with a crime in another state is a NCIC (National Crime Information Center) message on a DCI (Division of Criminal Information) terminal. Such a message by itself is sufficient basis for the magistrate to find that the fugitive is charged in the other state. Although a message should not appear on NCIC unless the warrant is outstanding in one state and the other state intends to extradite, the officer may want to confirm the NCIC message with someone in the other state before making an arrest.

Sometimes the officer's information that a person is a fugitive may come from another source, such as a telephone call, email, facsimile, or letter from an officer in another state. Such information can be used to determine whether the defendant is charged in the other state. In cases like these, as in cases in which an NCIC message is used, the other state should be asked to send a copy of the warrant or indictment as soon as possible so that it can be attached to the North Carolina warrant.

Another possibility, though unusual, is that the person has not yet been formally charged in the other state. For example, a person may have robbed a convenience store in Virginia late at night and fled to North Carolina, but no warrant was issued in the interim because a judicial official was not on duty in Virginia. The extradition statutes allow North Carolina officers to arrest fugitives in such cases but only after a North Carolina warrant has been issued, and that warrant may be issued only after the magistrate has made the same kind of finding of probable cause had the crime occurred in North Carolina. That is, the magistrate must find probable cause that

---

2. AOC-CR-910M is available at www.nccourts.org/Forms/Documents/169.pdf.

the defendant committed the crime in Virginia. The most likely basis for probable cause will be information relayed by Virginia officers through North Carolina officers. Once the warrant has been issued, the officer proceeds the same as in other fugitive cases mentioned above. (*Note*: Under G.S. 15A-403, an officer from another state contiguous to North Carolina has the authority to enter North Carolina when in hot pursuit of a person who allegedly committed an offense [usually limited to a felony] in the officer's state. After making an arrest, the officer must take the person to a North Carolina magistrate or other judicial official to begin the extradition process. For additional information, see page 17 of ROBERT L. FARB, ARREST, SEARCH, AND INVESTIGATION IN NORTH CAROLINA [4th ed. 2011].)

It may also be that the fugitive has already been convicted in the other state and has fled to avoid sentencing, has escaped, or has fled in violation of the conditions of the fugitive's probation, parole, or other post-release supervision. In such cases the magistrate simply determines that the fugitive was convicted and fled. The procedures are otherwise the same as for the person who has not yet been tried in the other state. However, in some cases the fugitive, as a condition of release on probation, parole, or post-release supervision, had previously waived extradition should he or she flee to another state—commonly known as a pre-signed waiver. (For example, North Carolina prisoners sign a waiver of extradition when released on parole or post-release supervision.) By entering into such an agreement, the probationer, parolee, or post-release supervisee has agreed in advance as a specific condition of release to waive the right to challenge the effort of any state to return him or her to the demanding state. In such a case, the procedures are simplified so that the other state may come to North Carolina to return the prisoner or probationer to that state.

There is another category of parolees, post-release supervisees, and probationers who may be retaken without involving the extradition process. Under the Interstate Compact for Adult Offender Supervision (ICAOS), of which all states and the District of Columbia are members, a parolee, post-release supervisee, or probationer may seek a transfer of supervision to another state. If the request is approved, the person's presence in the other state is not as a fugitive from justice (the typical ground for extradition) as set out in the extradition statutes because the person is lawfully in the other state. However, if the person while being supervised in the other state violates a condition of supervision or otherwise commits an act that permits or requires the sending state to seek the person's return, the compact has its own procedures outside the extradition process to retake the person to the sending state. These procedures ordinarily do not involve any court proceedings; any necessary hearings are conducted by a state's compact administrator or designee—see, for example, the procedures set out in G.S. 148-65.8. If the person is detained in the other state under the compact's procedures and brought before a judicial official, no bail is allowed pending a hearing conducted by the compact administrator or designee to determine if there is an appropriate basis for returning the person to the sending state. (*Note*: Even though the return of a person under the compact does not involve the extradition process, a person who seeks a transfer of supervision to another state is required to waive extradition from *any* state as a condition of the transfer.)

Once arrested, the fugitive is held until formal extradition procedures can take place. If the fugitive wishes to do so, he or she may waive extradition before a clerk or assistant clerk of superior court or a judge and be immediately released to the state from which he or she fled. Many fugitives choose to do this, knowing that they will be extradited and not wanting to spend the time required for formal extradition. The waiver must be in writing (use AOC-CR-912M, available through the N.C. Court System website[3]). Note that a fugitive may be tried for North Carolina criminal charges before being sent back to the demanding state.

If the fugitive does not waive extradition or had not previously executed a pre-signed waiver as a probationer, parolee, or post-release supervisee, the state from which the fugitive fled must formally request the governor of North Carolina to extradite. The request, based on information supplied by the prosecutor in the county where the crime was committed, will come from the governor of the other state. The extradition request to North Carolina includes a copy of the warrant or indictment against the fugitive, plus other paperwork establishing all the requirements of the normal extradition process. These papers are sent to the extradition secretary located in the North Carolina attorney general's office, which determines whether the paperwork is legally sufficient to justify extradition through issuance of a governor's warrant. The only questions the governor of North Carolina asks

---

3. AOC-CR-912M is available at www.nccourts.org/Forms/Documents/171.pdf.

in deciding whether to extradite are whether the fugitive is actually charged with a crime in another state and whether the person arrested in North Carolina is the fugitive. The governor's office does not attempt to determine whether there was probable cause for the charge; that is considered a matter between the other state and the fugitive—just like other defenses the fugitive might raise, such as self-defense or alibi.

If the attorney general's office on behalf of the governor is satisfied that the other state has met the requirements of extradition, a governor's warrant is issued. The warrant authorizes taking the fugitive into custody—the fugitive may actually already be in custody if he or she was not allowed bail or could not make bail—to be turned over to an agent of the other state. A fugitive who was released on bail is to be arrested pursuant to the warrant, and the bail is revoked. Before the fugitive is turned over to the other state, he or she must be taken before a judge to be informed of the right to challenge the legality of the arrest through habeas corpus proceedings and to have counsel appointed for that purpose if the fugitive cannot afford an attorney. The habeas corpus proceeding is held in North Carolina before a superior court judge. The only grounds for challenging the arrest under the governor's warrant are: (1) the person has not been charged with a crime in the other state or (2) he or she is not the person being sought. Because the grounds that can be raised are very limited, ten days is usually sufficient time in which to file a petition for a writ of habeas corpus. If the fugitive does not apply for a writ of habeas corpus, or tries to but fails, the fugitive is turned over to the agents from the other state. (The governor may recall the governor's warrant at his or her discretion, and this is occasionally done when new facts arise after the warrant was issued. The governor then may reissue the warrant if circumstances so indicate.)

Returning Fugitive Found in Another State to North Carolina

If a person who committed a crime in North Carolina flees to another state and is found there, essentially the same procedure takes place. A North Carolina fugitive may be extradited from another state if he or she committed any crime in this state, whether a felony or a misdemeanor. But the state pays the expenses of extradition only if the crime is a felony, escape (felony or misdemeanor), or a violation of probation, parole, or post-release supervision (for a felony or misdemeanor). The county pays for all other misdemeanors, and some other states are reluctant to extradite for minor crimes.

Once the fugitive is arrested in the other state, the North Carolina district attorney or assistant district attorney (the term *prosecutor* applies to both and will be used hereafter) of the county where the fugitive is charged is notified and must assemble the documents that the North Carolina extradition secretary will need in requesting extradition (assuming that the fugitive does not waive extradition or the other state refuses to honor any pre-signed waiver of extradition by a probationer, parolee, or post-release supervisee). These documents include copies of the arrest warrant with supporting affidavit (to support the warrant the affidavit *must* be dated before or on the same date of the issuance of the warrant) or indictment, a statement that the extradition is not sought to enforce a private claim, certain further information about the circumstances of the crime, and certifications that the documents are all true copies. The extradition secretary requires additional information, such as photographs, fingerprints, or a physical description. The extradition secretary reviews the materials to be sure they comply with the requirements of the other state and then, at the direction of the governor, formally requests extradition from that state. Once extradition is granted, the governor commissions one or more North Carolina officers named by the prosecutor of the prosecutorial district from which the fugitive fled to return the fugitive.

Fugitive from North Carolina Found in Another State

Crimes Subject to Extradition

Any person who is charged with a crime in North Carolina and flees to another state may be extradited to North Carolina to stand trial. (Also subject to extradition are those people who have been *convicted* in North Carolina and have escaped or have violated the conditions of probation, parole, or post-release supervision). But G.S. 15A-744 provides that the state of North Carolina is to pay the expenses of extradition only when the fugitive is charged with a felony or has violated the conditions of probation, parole, or post-release supervision—whether felony or misdemeanor. The state will also pay the expenses of extraditing a person who has escaped, whether the escape is a felony or misdemeanor. Thus a fugitive charged with a misdemeanor may be extradited, but in most cases the costs of that procedure (the greatest expense is sending an agent to return the fugitive) must be paid by the county where the crime was committed. For that reason extradition should never be initiated against someone charged with a misdemeanor unless there is some assurance that the county will pay the expenses.

Extradition may be sought for non-fugitives—those who commit acts while in another state intentionally resulting in a crime in North Carolina. For example, Peter Smith lives in Florida and conspires with Linda Jones to transport drugs to North Carolina, only Jones delivers the drugs but Smith never appears in North Carolina. Non-fugitive extraditions are discretionary with the governor of the other state.

The National Association of Extradition Officials recommends the policies set out below on extradition for certain offenses. The law allows extradition for each of the offenses mentioned, but the governor's office agrees with the recommended policies and expects all law enforcement officers and prosecutors to follow them.

Nonsupport. For abandonment and nonsupport, nonsupport of child born out of wedlock, and all similar offenses, action should first be taken under Chapter 52C of the General Statutes, the Uniform Interstate Family Support Act (UIFSA). Only if that procedure has failed should extradition be requested. If the UIFSA procedure has not been used, the extradition request should include an affidavit from the prosecutor or the appropriate law enforcement officer explaining fully the reason for not using UIFSA.

Child custody. Before seeking extradition for a violation of G.S. 14-320.1 (transporting a child out of state with intent to violate a custody order) a prosecutor should require the legal custodian of the child to pursue all available civil remedies. If there is a competing child custody order in another state, extradition will not be requested by the governor's office.

Worthless checks. Extradition should not be sought for violations of G.S. 14-107, writing worthless checks, unless the check or aggregate checks total more than $500 or the defendant is a chronic violator. These limitations do not apply if the charge under G.S. 14-107 is for writing a check on a nonexistent account or on a closed account. Nor is there any limit on extradition for forgery and similar offenses.

Removing mortgaged property. Only in exceptional circumstances should extradition be sought for violations of G.S. 14-114 (fraudulent disposal of personal property on which there is a security interest), G.S. 14-115 (secreting property to hinder enforcement of lien or security interest), or similar statutes. The amount of money involved in such a case does not alter the policy. Generally these problems should be handled as civil matters, especially if the defendant has made regular payments on the merchandise and now owes only a small balance. But if the defendant purchased a vehicle or other merchandise and immediately left North Carolina, making no payments whatsoever, there would appear to be intent to defraud and extradition may be sought.

Rental property. If a person fails to return rented property, such as an automobile, and the car has been found, there would appear to be no intent to steal and this matter should be handled civilly rather than through extradition. But if the person immediately leaves North Carolina for parts

Typical Process When Fugitive from North Carolina Is Found in Another State

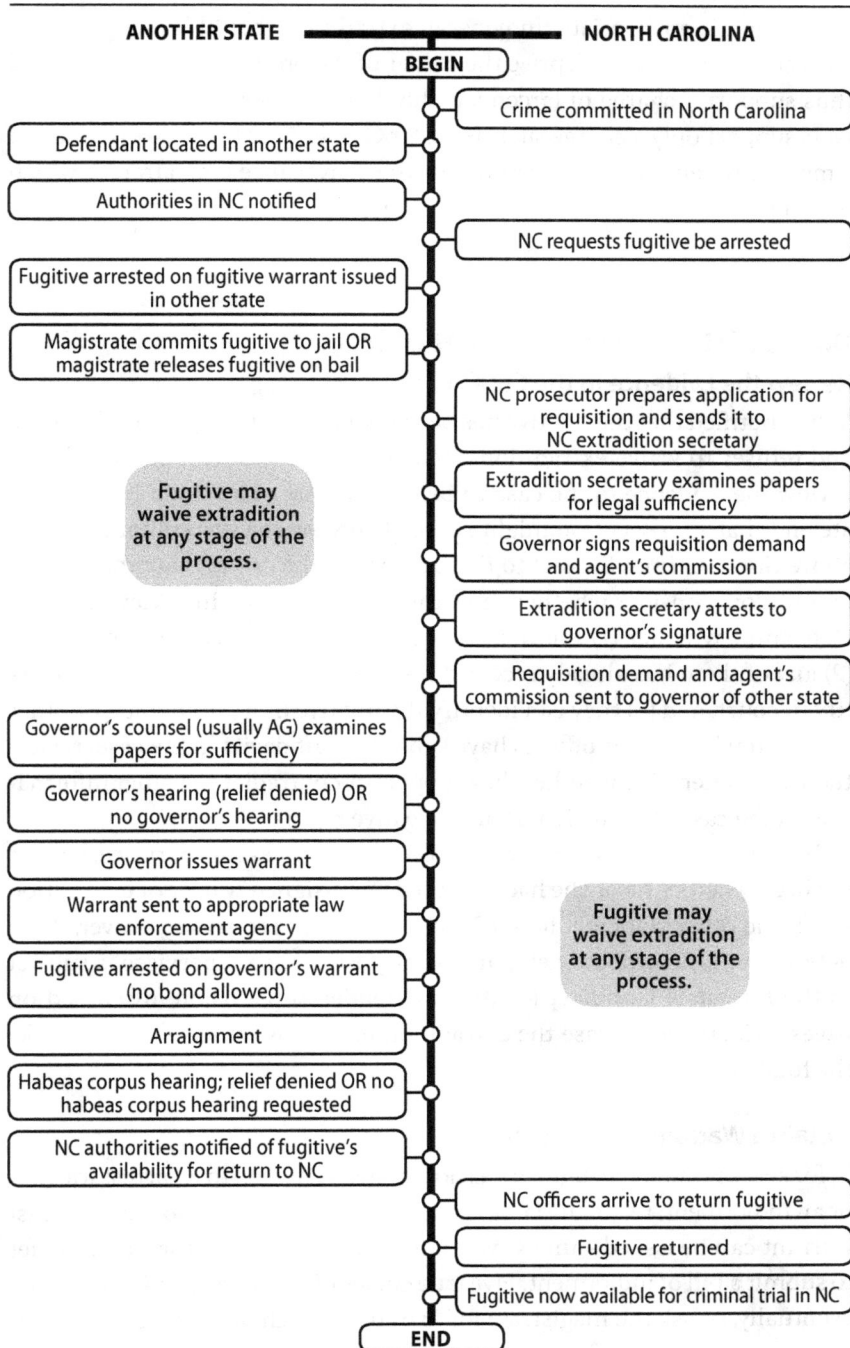

ANOTHER STATE ━━━━━━━━━━━━━━━ **NORTH CAROLINA**

BEGIN

Crime committed in North Carolina

Defendant located in another state

Authorities in NC notified

NC requests fugitive be arrested

Fugitive arrested on fugitive warrant issued in other state

Magistrate commits fugitive to jail OR magistrate releases fugitive on bail

NC prosecutor prepares application for requisition and sends it to NC extradition secretary

Extradition secretary examines papers for legal sufficiency

Fugitive may waive extradition at any stage of the process.

Governor signs requisition demand and agent's commission

Extradition secretary attests to governor's signature

Requisition demand and agent's commission sent to governor of other state

Governor's counsel (usually AG) examines papers for sufficiency

Governor's hearing (relief denied) OR no governor's hearing

Governor issues warrant

Warrant sent to appropriate law enforcement agency

Fugitive may waive extradition at any stage of the process.

Fugitive arrested on governor's warrant (no bond allowed)

Arraignment

Habeas corpus hearing; relief denied OR no habeas corpus hearing requested

NC authorities notified of fugitive's availability for return to NC

NC officers arrive to return fugitive

Fugitive returned

Fugitive now available for criminal trial in NC

END

unknown with rented property, larceny is probably the proper charge and extradition is appropriate. In general, extradition should be sought if the facts show an intent to deprive the owner of the property permanently and thus support a charge of larceny; it should not be sought, however, if the facts support only a charge such as under G.S. 14-72.2 (unauthorized use of a motor-propelled conveyance), unless the conveyance is an aircraft, which is a felony.

Duties of the Law Enforcement Officer

Review the Evidence in the Case

When notified that the fugitive has been taken into custody in another state and refuses to waive extradition, the law enforcement officer should first review the evidence in the case to be certain that extradition is appropriate and that a prosecution might succeed. Review the section immediately above titled "Crimes Subject to Extradition." If the crime is appropriate for extradition, consider whether the witnesses need to be interviewed again. Determine whether (1) the witnesses are likely to change their testimony, (2) any of them has already received restitution, (3) they are willing to testify in court, and (4) they can identify the fugitive by a photograph or other means. If witnesses or officers have submitted affidavits in the case, review these and determine whether they support or contradict the other information in the case. Also review all investigative reports.

If the fugitive is a probationer, parolee, or post-release supervisee, be sure to check whether he or she had executed a pre-signed waiver of extradition and if the other state will honor North Carolina's pre-signed waiver. Also, determine if the probationer, parolee, or post-release supervisee is subject to the Interstate Compact for Adult Offender Supervision (discussed on pages 4–5), in which case the extradition process is unnecessary to retake the fugitive.

Obtain a Warrant if Necessary

If, for some reason, the fugitive has not yet been charged in an arrest warrant or an indictment, relate the facts in the case to a magistrate so that an arrest warrant can be issued—unless you know that the prosecutor would prefer to submit a bill of indictment. Five true copies of the warrant will be needed eventually, so ask the magistrate for five copies, each one signed separately.

If a warrant or indictment has already been issued (which is usually the case), have a copy available for reference when you talk with the prosecutor. If the charging document is a warrant rather than an indictment, it must be accompanied by an affidavit (usually by the investigating officer or the victim before the same magistrate or judge signing the warrant) that states the basis for issuing the warrant. This affidavit must be sworn to before a magistrate or judge and should have the same date as the warrant (or earlier). Some states will not extradite if the date of the affidavit (for example, January 25, 2013) is later than the date on which the arrest warrant was issued (for example, January 20, 2013). Therefore, when a warrant has been issued without an accompanying affidavit (oral sworn testimony is sufficient to support an arrest warrant in North Carolina), a new arrest warrant must be issued when the affidavit is prepared so that the dates of the arrest warrant and the affidavit will be the same.

Before an officer enters the warrant on NCIC (National Crime Information Center), he or she should verify with a prosecutor that the district attorney's office is willing to extradite the fugitive. Meeting with a prosecutor is discussed below.

Check the Fugitive's Criminal Record

Check the fugitive's criminal record and bring a copy to your meeting with the prosecutor.

Meet with the Prosecutor

Bring the prosecutor all the information and documents discussed above. Be candid about any problems you foresee with witnesses or with the methods of investigation in the case and any other factor that might affect its outcome. At this meeting the prosecutor should decide whether to proceed with extradition. Usually he or she will then take responsibility for preparing the proper papers, but the prosecutor may ask for your assistance. If so, review the section of this manual titled "Checklist of Documents Needed for an Extradition Request."

Fugitive from North Carolina Found in Another State

Duties of the Law Enforcement Officer

1. Review the evidence in the case.
2. Obtain a warrant if necessary.
3. Check the fugitive's criminal record.
4. Meet with prosecutor.

Duties of the Prosecutor

1. Decide whether to seek extradition.
2. Prepare the proper papers for extradition.
3. Select agents to go to the other state.

Duties of the Clerk of Court

1. Certify papers for extradition.
2. Certify various officials who certify documents.

Duties of the Agent Sent to Bring the Fugitive Back

1. A male agent must return a male fugitive; a female agent, a female fugitive.
2. Wait for notification from the other state that authorities are ready to hand over the fugitive; arrange to take custody at earliest possible date following notification.
3. Receive approval for reimbursement expenses before going to the other state.
4. Upon return to North Carolina, have the sheriff of the county where the fugitive is to be tried complete the part of the extradition commission form indicating that the prisoner has been received.
5. Complete the return portion of the commission form and submit it to the extradition secretary. (If the fugitive could not be brought back, that fact must be stated on the return portion of the commission and an explanation given.)
6. If the fugitive decided to waive extradition, send a copy of that waiver to the extradition secretary.

Duties of the Prosecutor

Decide Whether to Seek Extradition

After a law enforcement officer has been notified that a fugitive from North Carolina is in custody in another state and refuses to waive extradition, the officer should come to you with the relevant information (see the previous section titled "Duties of the Law Enforcement Officer"). You must decide whether extradition should be sought. First, review the section of this manual titled "Crimes Subject to Extradition." If you are satisfied that extradition is appropriate for the kind of offense with which the fugitive has been charged, next consider the following factors:

- the seriousness of the offense;
- the evidence available to prove the crime;
- the challenges that might be mounted against the evidence or the methods of investigation;
- the defendant's character, including prior convictions;
- the probability that the defendant will commit similar crimes elsewhere;
- the probable length of time the defendant will be imprisoned if returned to North Carolina and convicted and the effect of that imprisonment on his or her conduct after release;
- whether, in child abduction and nonsupport cases, civil remedies are more effective or appropriate than extradition;
- whether the fugitive is charged with a crime in the other state and may face a substantial prison term if convicted;
- the cost of having the defendant returned to North Carolina;
- whether, in worthless check cases, the amount of money involved justifies extradition;
- the effect of not extraditing on others in the community who might consider committing similar crimes;
- the need to act quickly because the other state may be considering whether to release the fugitive on bond.

Prepare the Proper Papers for Extradition

First review the section of this manual titled "Checklist of Documents Needed for an Extradition Request," which lists the documents that must be submitted to the extradition secretary on behalf of the governor. An administrative assistant may prepare these documents, and a law enforcement officer may assist. The application for requisition may be signed by a prosecutor.

If the fugitive has not yet been charged in North Carolina in an arrest warrant or indictment, the next step is to have such a process issued. Although an arrest warrant is sufficient, proceedings in the other state usually go faster when an indictment is used, so an indictment should be sought if possible. If an indictment is used, include an order for arrest. If an arrest warrant is used, it must be accompanied by an affidavit (usually by the investigating officer or the victim) that states the grounds for charging the defendant. This affidavit must be sworn to before a magistrate or judge and should have the same date as the warrant (or earlier). Some states will not extradite if the date of the affidavit (for example, January 25, 2013) is later than the date of the arrest warrant (for example, January 20, 2013). Therefore, when a warrant has been issued without an accompanying affidavit (oral sworn testimony is sufficient to support an arrest warrant in North Carolina), a new arrest warrant must be issued when the affidavit is prepared so that the dates of the arrest warrant and the affidavit will be the same.

The fugitive warrant served on the fugitive by the other state will provide judicial restraint of the fugitive for only thirty days, with extensions up to an additional sixty days. The additional sixty days is discretionary with the other state's judge. Therefore, the district attorney's office should not delay in requesting extradition so that a governor's warrant can be issued and served on the fugitive.

Select the Agents to Go to the Other State

The application for requisition is to include the names of the agents who will go to the other state to return the fugitive. It is best to have the investigating officers or other officers who are familiar with the case named as agents. It is required that an *individual* be named as an agent, and that person must have the option of naming someone else. For example, the appointment might read: "Sheriff John Smith of (*name county*) and/or his agent." North Carolina and many other states require that a female agent be named when the fugitive to be returned is a woman and a male agent for a male fugitive. Agents are expected to be ready at any time to travel to the other state when extradition has been granted by the other state or when a hearing is to be held there. The state does not pay travel expenses for a hearing unless the fugitive is returned on that trip. After being notified by the other state that the fugitive is available to be returned to North Carolina, the prosecutor should review the section of this manual titled "Duties of the Agent Sent to Bring the Fugitive Back."

Duties of the Clerk of Court

The clerk of court has only a limited role in bringing a fugitive back to North Carolina. When a prosecutor makes the request for extradition to the Governor of North Carolina (who will in turn make the same request to the governor of the state where the fugitive is located), he or she includes various documents, including a copy of the arrest warrant or indictment. Each document must be certified by the official who issued it or by the keeper of the original, the clerk of court. Also, the clerk must certify that the various other officials who certify the documents—the prosecutor, magistrate, or judge—are indeed the officials they claim to be. In turn, a judge must certify that the clerk is indeed the clerk. A summary of the documents and certifications needed for the extradition request is included in the section of this manual titled "Checklist of Documents Needed for an Extradition Request." Otherwise, the clerk has no duties in connection with extradition of a North Carolina fugitive from another state.

Duties of the Agent Sent to Bring the Fugitive Back

When a prosecutor applies to the Governor of North Carolina to seek the extradition of a fugitive who is in another state, he or she names the law enforcement officer(s) to be designated the governor's agents for bringing the fugitive back. There must be a male agent to return a male fugitive and a female agent to return a female fugitive. An officer who has been designated an agent should not go to the other state until he or she has been notified that the governor of that state has approved extradition and the authorities there are ready to hand over the fugitive. Officers seeking reimbursement of expenses from the Extradition/Fugitive Section of the North Carolina Department of Public Safety must receive approval from the section before going to the other state to return the fugitive. (The current reimbursement form is reproduced in the appendix.)

An agent should arrange to take custody of the fugitive in the other state at the earliest possible date following notification that the fugitive is ready to be surrendered. While federal law (18 U.S.C. § 3182) implies that a fugitive is to remain in custody in the other state for at least thirty days to await the arrival of agents from the demanding state, local jurisdictions frequently require agents to appear in a much shorter time.

Your commission as an agent of the Governor of North Carolina will be sent to the other state along with the governor's request for extradition and will be waiting for you there. When you return the fugitive to the North Carolina county where he or she is to be tried, the sheriff should complete the part of the commission form indicating that the prisoner has been received. You must complete the return portion of the commission and submit it to the extradition secretary. If for some reason the fugitive could not be brought back, that fact must be stated on the return portion of the commission and an explanation given.

If the fugitive decided to waive extradition, the officer who brought the fugitive back must send a copy of that waiver to the extradition secretary.

Checklist of Documents Needed for an Extradition Request

All of the documents that might be needed when a request for extradition is sent to the extradition secretary are presented in the sidebar on page 19. Usually a prosecutor is responsible for gathering the documents, though in some districts the prosecutor may have substantial assistance from an administrative assistant, a law enforcement officer, or someone else. The list states when a document must be certified or signed by a particular person. Whoever gathers the documents should collect *five* complete sets, four to go to the extradition secretary and one to be retained in the prosecutor's files.

When there is more than one charge, the person who prepares the request should base the request on the strongest charge. Once the fugitive is returned, he or she may be charged with any number of offenses. That charges were not included in the request for extradition does not mean they are waived.

Checklist of Documents Needed for an Extradition Request

Arrest warrant with affidavit or indictment with order for arrest

Certification of documents

Certifications of office

Application for requisition

Certification of the prosecutor

Special affidavits for certain offenses

Photograph and fingerprints of the fugitive

Copies of statute the fugitive is charged with violating

Arrest Warrant or Indictment

A copy of the arrest warrant is needed if the fugitive has not yet been indicted. If the fugitive has been indicted, the arrest warrant is not needed; a copy of the indictment along with an order for arrest will be used instead. The warrant or indictment should be reviewed to make sure it properly charges the offense and cites the statute violated. Use of an indictment simplifies the process. An order for arrest is not sufficient by itself.

Affidavit Supporting the Arrest Warrant

When the charging document is an arrest warrant, it must be supported by an affidavit. The most likely person to write the affidavit is the investigating officer or the victim. The affidavit must state enough facts to establish probable cause for the issuance of the warrant. Also, to avoid questions in the other state concerning the authority of the official to issue the warrant, the affidavit must be sworn to before a magistrate or judge rather than a clerk or notary. To show that the affidavit was the basis for issuing the warrant, the affidavit must be dated before or on the same date of the warrant. Some states will not extradite if the date of the affidavit (for example, January 25, 2013) shows that it was issued after the date on which the arrest warrant was issued (for example, January 20, 2013). Therefore, when a warrant has been issued without an accompanying affidavit (oral sworn testimony is sufficient to support an arrest warrant in North Carolina), a new arrest warrant must be issued so that the dates of the arrest warrant and the affidavit will be legally sufficient.

An affidavit is clearly not necessary when the charging document is an indictment, though a few other states prefer also to have an affidavit or warrant, or both.

Certification of Documents

If a warrant and affidavit are submitted, they must be accompanied by a certification of the magistrate or judge who issued the warrant or took the affidavit. A clerk of court may certify copies of these documents when he or she is the keeper of the originals. Each copy must be certified.

Certifications of Office

When a judge or magistrate certifies a document, the clerk of court must certify that person's official character. Then a district court or superior court judge must certify the official character of the clerk. And in turn the clerk must certify the official character of the judge who certified the clerk.

Indictment

If the fugitive has been indicted, the indictment should be submitted rather than the arrest warrant. The prosecutor should make certain that the indictment properly charges the offense and has been signed by the foreperson. An order for arrest must accompany the indictment. The prosecutor should also check to make sure it cites the statute violated. The authenticity of each copy must be certified by the clerk of court, the official character of the clerk certified by the judge, and the official character of the judge certified by the clerk.

Application for Requisition

This form (GOV. 1, available through the N.C. Court System website[4]) must be filled out in full. Note that it includes the following information:

- The fugitive's full name, properly spelled. Include any aliases.
- A statement that in the prosecutor's opinion the ends of public justice require that the fugitive be brought to North Carolina for trial.

---

4. GOV. 1 is available at www.nccourts.org/Forms/Documents/736.pdf.

- A statement that the prosecutor believes that there is sufficient evidence to convict the fugitive.
- The names and addresses of the agents who are to bring the fugitive back to North Carolina from the other state and a statement that the persons recommended as agents are proper persons and have no private interest in the arrest or conviction of the fugitive.
- A statement whether there has been any earlier application for requisition of the same person for the same transaction, including the date of such request, and a statement of the reason for the present request if there was an earlier one.
- If the fugitive is under arrest in the other state, a statement that the fugitive is under arrest, the nature of the proceedings, and the place (with complete address) where he or she is in custody, if known. If the fugitive is out on bail, the date of his or her hearing should be stated. If the fugitive's home or business address is known, that should be stated also along with the source of this information.
- A statement that the application is not made for the purpose of enforcing the collection of a debt or for any private purpose whatever and that if the requisition is granted the criminal proceeding will not be used for any such purposes.
- A statement of the crime charged and the approximate time, date, places, and circumstances of its occurrence. This statement should include a citation to the statute violated.
- A statement that the person was in North Carolina when the crime was committed and has since fled. Or if the person committed an act in another state that intentionally resulted in the crime in North Carolina, that fact must be stated.
- If the crime did not occur recently, an explanation for the delay in making an application.

The requisition form provides blanks for all this information or notes the need to include the information. (*Note*: If the prosecutor is seeking extradition for a non-fugitive, form GOV. 1 should be modified to reflect the wording "the accused" instead of "the fugitive," and 9b. must be used instead of 9a.)

Certification of the Prosecutor

The clerk must certify the official character of the prosecutor who submits the application, and in turn the clerk must be certified by a judge, who must then be certified by the clerk. Note that only one such certification of official character per official is required, no matter how many documents that official has signed.

Special Affidavits

In any case involving fraud, false pretense, embezzlement, felony child support, or forgery, there must also be an affidavit of the principal complaining witness or informant that (a) the application is made in good faith for the sole purpose of criminal punishment and (b) he or she does not desire or expect to use the prosecution for the purpose of collecting a debt or for any other private purpose, either directly or indirectly. If such an affidavit is not included, a good explanation for its absence must be given.

Photograph and Fingerprints of the Fugitive

One of the legal issues that may be raised at a habeas corpus hearing is the identity of the fugitive. Many states require some identification of the fugitive. Therefore, a requisition request should be accompanied by fingerprints, a photograph, and/or a physical description. Although a photograph is not required, it can be very helpful in identification and should be included whenever possible. It should be accompanied by an affidavit to the effect that the person shown is the person charged with the crime. Fingerprints are not required, but they should be provided for identification when available.

The Statute the Fugitive Is Charged with Violating

A copy of the statute the fugitive is charged with violating should be included.

When the Fugitive Has Escaped from Custody or Violated Probation, Parole, or Post-Release Supervision

Extradition procedures are slightly different when the fugitive from North Carolina has already been convicted in this state and has escaped from custody or has left the state in violation of parole, probation, or post-release supervision conditions—assuming that the fugitive cannot be returned based on a pre-signed waiver by a probationer, parolee, or post-release supervisee discussed in the "Introduction" to this manual. A separate form, GOV. 2 (available from the N.C. Court System website[5]), is used for requisition in these cases. The application is to be made by the prosecutor or the sheriff if the person was in jail awaiting transfer to the Department of Public Safety or if he or she was out of jail pending appeal. If the person escaped from the Department of Public Safety's custody, the application is to be made by the secretary of public safety or a properly designated official of the department. For a fugitive who left the state in violation of probation conditions, the application may be made by the prosecutor of the district where the person was serving probation (or it might be prepared for the prosecutor's signature by the appropriate state official). If the person was on parole or post-release supervision, the request may be made by either the prosecutor or the Post-Release Supervision and Parole Commission. The application for requisition is to be accompanied by the following documents:

- (All cases) Indictment (or arrest warrant, if the person was tried on a warrant) for original charge of which the defendant was convicted.

---

5. GOV. 2 is available at www.nccourts.org/Forms/Documents/189.pdf.

- (Escape) The judgment of conviction and sentence on which the person was being held when he or she escaped.
- (Escape) Indictment or arrest warrant and affidavit for escape or an affidavit of the officer from whose custody the person escaped, showing that an escape occurred and the circumstances of it.
- (Escape) The record of escape, which includes the transcript and fingerprints.
- (Probation) Probation judgment, probation violation report, and order for arrest.
- (Parole or post-release supervision) Judgment of conviction and sentence and documents granting parole or post-release supervision and revocation of parole or post-release supervision.

Five copies of each document should be prepared; four are sent to the extradition secretary, and one is retained by the official who made the application. The clerk of court who holds the original must certify to the authenticity of the indictment (or warrant) and the judgment of conviction and sentence. The clerk must also certify the official character of the person who made the affidavit that describes the fugitive's escape. The official character of the clerk must be certified by a judge and vice versa.

Extradition of Military Personnel

If extradition is requested for someone who is on active duty with the air force, army, marine corps, or navy, the application must be accompanied by an agreement by the appropriate authorities that:

- The fugitive's commanding officer will be informed of the outcome of any trial and
- If the military authorities desire his or her return, the fugitive will, if acquitted or when his or her sentence is completed, be returned to the military authorities at the place where the fugitive was taken into custody or taken to the nearest receiving ship, station, or barracks at the expense of the authority that seeks the requisition.

If the crime is a felony and the requisition is made through the governor's office, this agreement will be prepared by the governor's office and the state will pay the expenses. If the crime is a misdemeanor, so that the expenses of extradition are to be borne by the county, then the prosecutor or other official who applies for the requisition must prepare and execute the agreement. The agreement may be in the form of a letter to the secretary of the appropriate branch of the service, setting out the required promises. See the example of such an agreement in the appendix.

Executive Agreements

An executive agreement may be entered into between governors and should be used instead of the Interstate Agreement on Detainers (IAD) (discussed on pages 61–62) when an inmate serving an active sentence in another state is charged with a crime in North Carolina for which the prosecutor is seeking the death penalty. The agreement may set out which state will keep a prisoner depending on the sentence to be imposed if there is a conviction, and it may set out the order of prosecutions of a prisoner by two states.

An executive agreement is prepared by the district attorney's office and forwarded to the governor along with the application for requisition. The crucial promise in an executive agreement is that the fugitive will be returned to the other state upon demand, immediately after the trial is completed in North Carolina. A trial is considered completed when the defendant is sentenced, not when the appellate process is completed.

(*Note*: When the conviction occurs in North Carolina, the inmate should be returned to the other state unless the executive agreement states otherwise. Do not place the fugitive with the North Carolina Department of Public Safety as a North Carolina inmate. Although executive agreements usually provide for the fugitive's return, they are flexible instruments that can be tailored to fit particular circumstances.)

Other Special Cases

Fugitives Outside of the United States

International extradition is governed by individual treaties, and the documentary requirements as well as the types of extraditable offenses vary. In cases of international extradition, the prosecutor completes the same papers and sends the application to the Office of International Affairs at the U.S. Department of Justice in Washington. The extradition secretary should be contacted before seeking an international extradition and provided with a copy of any extradition request sent to the U.S. Department of Justice.

Juveniles

When a juvenile has been charged with a crime in North Carolina and leaves the state, the juvenile may be returned under formal extradition proceedings. If at least sixteen years old when the crime was committed and brought back as an adult, the juvenile must be tried as an adult. Extradition may not be needed to return a juvenile. The Interstate Compact for Juveniles (G.S. 7B-4000 through -4002) provides a procedure for the return of runaways, escapees, and juveniles charged as delinquent for a violation of a criminal law. The compact also provides for out-of-state supervision of delinquent probationers and parolees. See the discussion under the section in this manual titled "Return of Juveniles under Interstate Compact for Juveniles."

Fugitives on Indian Reservations

If the fugitive is located on an Indian reservation, the prosecutor completes the same papers and sends the application to the extradition secretary. The governor's office will process the request, add its endorsement, and send it to the governor of the state in which the reservation is physically located.

Fugitives in United States Possessions

If the fugitive is in a U.S. territory, the prosecutor completes the same papers and sends the application to the extradition secretary. The governor's office will process the request, add its endorsement, and send it directly to the territorial governor.

Fugitives in the District of Columbia

If the fugitive is in the District of Columbia, the prosecutor completes the same papers and sends the application to the extradition secretary. The governor's office will process the request, add its endorsement, and send it to the chief judge of the Superior Court of the District of Columbia. The District of Columbia has several special requirements for extradition. One requirement is that the fugitive must be identified by photograph or other description or by sending a witness who can identify him or her. The District of Columbia is also very strict in requiring a timely application; the application should not be delayed.

Renewal of the Application

When an application must be renewed—for example, when the fugitive could not be found in the state from which requisition was first sought—new or recertified copies of the papers required for extradition must be furnished.

Fugitive from Another State Found In North Carolina

Duties of the Arresting Officer
Before an Arrest Is Made

Determine whether the person is a fugitive. The first thing the officer needs to know is whether the suspect is charged with a crime in another state (by warrant or indictment) or has escaped from imprisonment there (following a conviction) or has violated probation, parole, or post-release supervision by leaving that state. An officer usually learns that someone is a fugitive by receiving an NCIC message on the DCI terminal, less often by telephone, letter, facsimile, or email from an officer in the other state. The DCI message by itself is sufficient to obtain a North Carolina arrest warrant for the fugitive, but the information should be verified by phone or otherwise if possible. As mentioned below, a copy of the other state's warrant or indictment should be obtained as soon as possible and attached to the North Carolina warrant. If the fugitive violated probation, parole, or post-release supervision by leaving that state, the officer should verify whether the fugitive had signed a pre-signed waiver of extradition (discussed in the "Introduction" to this manual).

Determine whether to arrest with or without a North Carolina warrant. If the fugitive has been formally charged with a crime in the other state and the crime is punishable in that state by death or imprisonment for more than one year, the fugitive may be arrested without a North Carolina warrant. Otherwise, an arrest may not be made until a North Carolina magistrate has issued a warrant. It is always preferable to obtain a warrant first if time allows.

If the Arrest Is to Be Made without a Warrant

First, *arrest the fugitive* following the same procedure used when making an arrest for a North Carolina crime. Tell the fugitive why he or she has been arrested.

Take the fugitive to a magistrate. This requirement is the same as when an officer makes an arrest for a North Carolina crime.

Tell the magistrate the reason for the arrest. The officer tells the magistrate why he or she believes the person has been charged with a crime in another state. If the reason is a DCI message, letter, facsimile, or email, a copy of that record should be given to the magistrate to be attached to the fugitive affidavit (AOC-CR-911M, available through the N.C. Court System website[6]). The magistrate is to determine only whether the person has been formally charged in the other state, not whether there is probable cause to believe the fugitive actually committed the crime. In this case, because the person was arrested without a warrant, the magistrate must also determine that the crime is punishable by death or imprisonment for more than one year.

Take the fugitive to jail or release on bail as ordered by the magistrate. Unless the crime is punishable by death or life imprisonment or the fugitive had executed a pre-signed waiver of extradition as a probationer, parolee, or post-release supervisee, the magistrate may release a fugitive on bail with sufficient sureties just as if he or she were charged with a North Carolina crime.

Request a copy of the warrant or indictment from the other state. If this has not already been done, the arresting officer should ask his or her contact in the other state for a copy of the arrest warrant or indictment charging the fugitive with the crime there or a copy of the pre-signed waiver of extradition executed by the fugitive probationer, parolee, or post-release supervisee. When the copy arrives, attach it to the magistrate's order (AOC-CR-909M, available through the N.C. Court System website[7]).

---

6. AOC-CR-911M is available at www.nccourts.org/Forms/Documents/170.pdf.
7. AOC-CR-909M is available at www.nccourts.org/Forms/Documents/168.pdf.

Typical Process When Fugitive from Another State Is Found in North Carolina

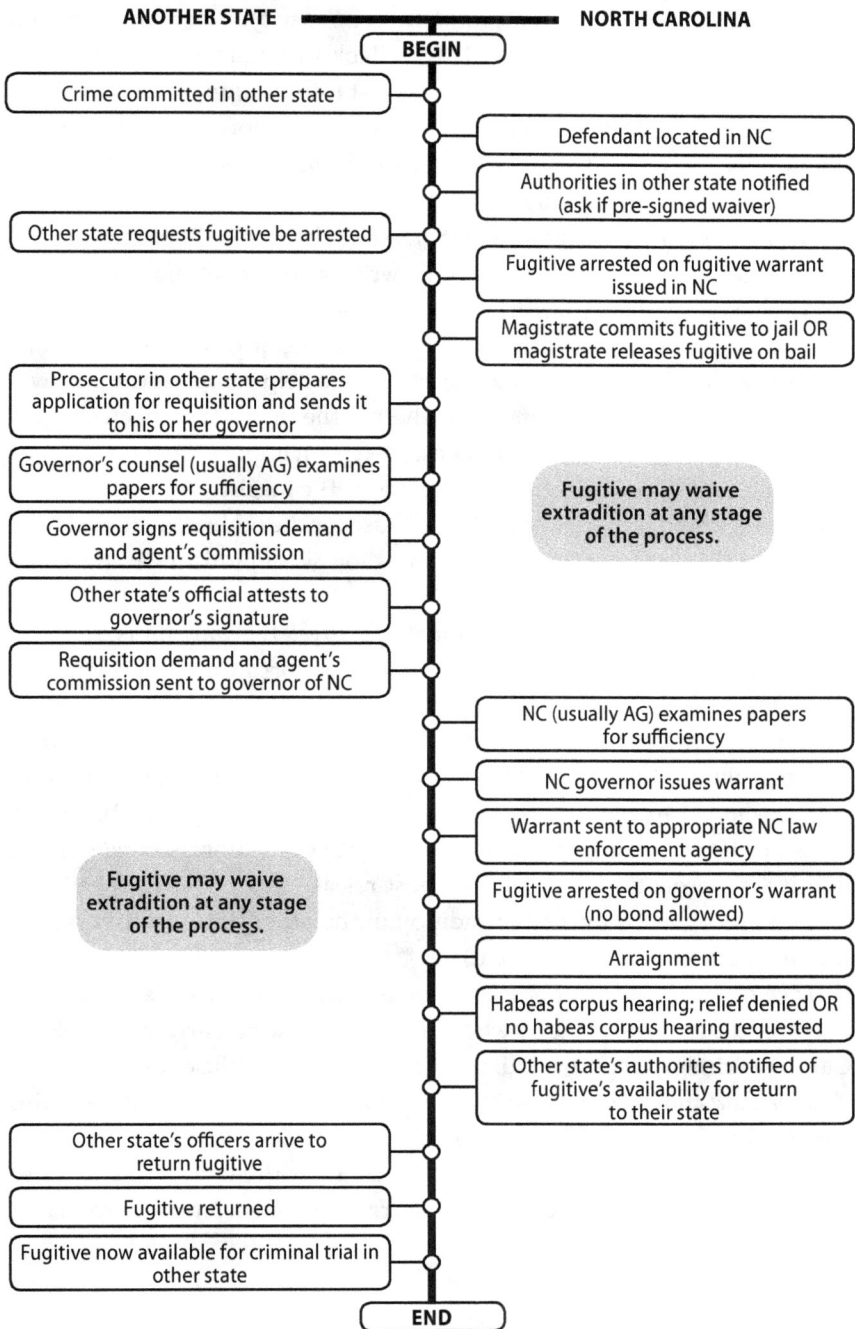

ANOTHER STATE ━━━━━ **NORTH CAROLINA**

BEGIN

Crime committed in other state

Defendant located in NC

Authorities in other state notified (ask if pre-signed waiver)

Other state requests fugitive be arrested

Fugitive arrested on fugitive warrant issued in NC

Magistrate commits fugitive to jail OR magistrate releases fugitive on bail

Prosecutor in other state prepares application for requisition and sends it to his or her governor

Governor's counsel (usually AG) examines papers for sufficiency

Fugitive may waive extradition at any stage of the process.

Governor signs requisition demand and agent's commission

Other state's official attests to governor's signature

Requisition demand and agent's commission sent to governor of NC

NC (usually AG) examines papers for sufficiency

NC governor issues warrant

Warrant sent to appropriate NC law enforcement agency

Fugitive may waive extradition at any stage of the process.

Fugitive arrested on governor's warrant (no bond allowed)

Arraignment

Habeas corpus hearing; relief denied OR no habeas corpus hearing requested

Other state's authorities notified of fugitive's availability for return to their state

Other state's officers arrive to return fugitive

Fugitive returned

Fugitive now available for criminal trial in other state

END

If a Warrant Is to Be Obtained before an Arrest Is Made

First, *go to the magistrate and complete an affidavit for an arrest warrant.* The fugitive affidavit (AOC-CR-911M, available through the N.C. Court System website[8]) contains instructions on what information is needed. Either the arresting officer or the magistrate may fill out the form, but the arresting officer must be certain that information on the form is accurate. The officer as well as the affiant must sign it.

Tell the magistrate your reason for arresting the fugitive. If you have a DCI message, letter, email, facsimile, or other written document showing that the fugitive has been charged with a crime in another state or has escaped from imprisonment there or violated probation, parole, or post-release supervision, show that document to the magistrate and help complete the affidavit. The magistrate is to determine only whether the fugitive has been charged with a crime in the other state or has escaped from imprisonment or violated probation, parole, or post-release supervision. The magistrate is not trying to determine whether there was probable cause for the other state to make the charge. In this case it is not necessary to show what punishment the other state places on the crime.

Once the warrant is issued, arrest the fugitive. The warrant is executed the same as if the person were charged with a North Carolina crime. Tell the fugitive the reason for his or her arrest.

Take the fugitive to a magistrate. This is the same procedure used when arresting with a warrant for a North Carolina crime. The magistrate is to decide whether to allow bail with sufficient sureties, except that bail is not allowed when the crime is punishable by death or life imprisonment or the fugitive is a probationer, parolee, or post-release supervisee who had executed a pre-signed waiver of extradition in the other state (as discussed in the "Introduction" to this manual).

Take the fugitive to jail or release on bail as ordered by the magistrate. The procedure is the same as when an officer makes an arrest for a North Carolina crime, except that bail must be made with sufficient sureties.

Request a copy of the warrant or indictment from the other state. If this has not already been done, ask your contact in the other state for a copy of the arrest warrant or indictment charging the fugitive with the crime there. When the copy arrives, attach it to the arrest warrant issued in North Carolina.

---

8. AOC-CR-911M is available at www.nccourts.org/Forms/Documents/170.pdf.

If the Fugitive Has Not Yet Been Charged in the Other State

The extradition statutes also allow an officer to arrest someone who has committed a crime in another state even if he or she has not yet been formally charged there. This situation should rarely occur. It is most likely to happen when someone commits a crime in a neighboring state and immediately flees to North Carolina and an officer is contacted before a judicial official has been found in that other state to issue the warrant.

Before making the arrest you must obtain a warrant for arrest from a magistrate. A standard North Carolina arrest warrant form may be used for this purpose but modified to allege (a) the name of the crime in the other state (without giving all the elements) and (b) the citation to the statute of the other state, if known. Because the other state has not yet issued a warrant, you must show the magistrate probable cause to believe the fugitive committed the crime in the other state, just as if you were requesting a warrant to arrest for a crime committed in North Carolina. Probable cause is usually provided by the information you received from officers in the other state linking the person with the crime there. Once the arrest warrant is issued, proceed just as if the warrant was charging a North Carolina crime. Ask the other state's officers to send a copy of the warrant issued there after the returning fugitive is charged in that state. When the copy arrives, attach it to the North Carolina arrest warrant.

If the Fugitive Had Executed a Pre-Signed Waiver of Extradition in the Other State

The National Association of Extradition Officials recognizes that the Uniform Criminal Extradition Act should be construed liberally so as to effectuate its purpose of making uniform the laws of those states that have adopted it, asserts that "pre-signed waivers of extradition are valid and should be recognized," and advises states to uniformly "enforce such pre-signed waivers of extradition."

A person in the other state may have been required to execute a pre-signed waiver of extradition as a condition of probation, parole, post-release supervision, or other type of release. Based on the provisions of the Uniform Criminal Extradition Act, pre-signed waivers of extradition executed as a condition of probation, parole, post-release supervision, or other type of release in another state are valid and effective under the Uniform Criminal Extradition Act to waive any rights to statutory extradition proceedings otherwise provided by the state of North Carolina and may be recognized according to the terms of the waiver. Thus formal extradition proceedings are not necessary to return probationers, parolees, post-release supervisees, and similar kinds of violators who have signed waivers of extradition as a condition of their release.

Once the other state's request has been made and the probationer, parolee, or post-release supervisee has been arrested, the arresting law enforcement agency should (1) make a prompt inquiry of the other state to determine whether a waiver was signed and (2) obtain a certified copy of the pre-signed waiver of extradition, properly establishing both the identity of the probationer, parolee, or post-release supervisee and the authority of the other state's officer. Upon receipt of this information, the law enforcement agency should make the fugitive available to the other state.

Duties of the Magistrate

If the Officer Comes to You before Arresting the Fugitive

Determine whether there are grounds for an arrest. Place the officer under oath and ask the reasons for making an arrest. The three grounds that justify an arrest are (1) the person is charged with a crime in another state and fled, (2) the person was convicted of a crime in another state and has fled to avoid sentencing or has escaped from imprisonment there, and (3) the person was convicted of a crime in another state and violated the conditions of probation, parole, or post-release supervision by fleeing. The officer's information must be reliable. Usually it will consist of a DCI message, but it could be a letter, facsimile, email, or phone call from an officer in the other state or even a copy of the warrant or indictment from the other state. The magistrate's duty is not to determine whether there is probable cause to believe the person committed the crime, only whether the person is charged in the other state or has escaped and is the person wanted by the other state.

Complete the affidavit and arrest warrant. It is necessary to complete both the fugitive affidavit (AOC-CR-911M) and the fugitive warrant (AOC-CR-910M) (both available through the N.C. Court System website[9]) and be certain that they are attached. Follow the usual procedure concerning the number of copies to be completed, sending the original to the clerk of

---

9. AOC-CR-911M is available at www.nccourts.org/Forms/Documents/170.pdf; AOC-CR-910M, at www.nccourts.org/Forms/Documents/169.pdf.

court's office. Attach to the original the DCI message or any other document used to establish that the person is a fugitive. Remind the officer to obtain a copy of the arrest warrant or indictment in the other state as soon as possible and have it attached to the original copy of the warrant in the clerk's office.

If the Officer Brings in the Fugitive after Making an Arrest without a Warrant

Determine whether the officer had adequate grounds for the arrest. Place the officer under oath and ask the reasons for making the arrest. An officer may arrest without a warrant only when the person has been charged with a crime in another state and that crime is punishable by death or by imprisonment for more than one year. The person might have been charged in the other state by the issuance of an arrest warrant there, by an indictment, or by information filed by a prosecutor in that state. The magistrate's duty is only to determine whether the person has been charged in the other state, not whether there was probable cause for the charge. The officer's information that the person has been charged must be reliable. Usually it will be a DCI message, but it could be a letter, email, facsimile, or telephone call from an officer in the other state. Sometimes the officer may even have a copy of the warrant or indictment from the other state. If the information is a DCI message, ask the officer whether he or she has contacted the other state to verify that the charge is still outstanding and they wish to extradite. This verification is not essential—the DCI message is sufficient justification for arresting the fugitive—but it is a highly recommended practice. Of course you must determine also that the person arrested is the person charged in the other state.

Complete a magistrate's order. Complete the fugitive affidavit (AOC-CR-911M) and the magistrate's order (AOC-CR-909M) (both available from the N.C. Court System website[10]). Follow the usual procedure on the number of copies to be completed; the original goes to the clerk's office. Attach to the original the DCI message or other written document used to establish that the person is a fugitive. Remind the officer to obtain a copy of the other state's warrant or indictment as soon as possible and have it attached to the original copy of the magistrate's order in the clerk's office.

---

10. AOC-CR-911M is available at www.nccourts.org/Forms/Documents/170.pdf; AOC-CR-909M, at www.nccourts.org/Forms/Documents/168.pdf.

Inform the fugitive of the charges. Follow the same procedure you follow in any other case, informing the person of the charge, the right to communicate with counsel and friends, and whether the person is entitled to bail.

Determine whether to allow bail. G.S. 15A-736 allows a fugitive to be given bail unless the offense with which the fugitive is charged in the other state is punishable by death or life imprisonment. Apparently the only form of pretrial release that may be used is a bail bond with sureties. The bail bond schedule given the magistrate by the senior resident superior court judge may include instructions on what bond to set for fugitives. Sometimes the same amount is required as for a similar North Carolina crime, and sometimes that amount is doubled or otherwise multiplied. If bail is not allowed, or if the defendant cannot meet the bail, he or she should be committed to the county jail.

(*Note:* Bail is not allowed after (1) a governor's warrant has been issued, (2) the fugitive had executed a pre-signed waiver of extradition, typically as a probationer, parolee, or post-release supervisee, or (3) the person was transferred from another state to North Carolina under the Interstate Compact for Adult Offender Supervision (see discussion on pages 4–5) for supervision as a parolee, post-release supervisee, or probationer and the state under the compact seeks to retake the person and the person has been arrested or detained under the compact's procedures. A person taken into custody under the Interstate Compact for Adult Offender Supervision is not returned to a state under the extradition process, but the no-bail issue is mentioned here so that magistrates will have this information if such a person appears before them.)

Order the fugitive to appear in district court. Whether the fugitive is released on bond or cannot make bond or is ineligible for bail, the release or commitment order should direct that he or she appear before a district court judge at the earliest possible session of court. Although the statute does not require an immediate district court appearance for the fugitive who is released on bond, such an appearance will give the district judge an early opportunity to review the fugitive's bond, explain the extradition process, and appoint counsel if necessary. Fugitives often waive formal extradition once they are told about the process and have talked to a lawyer. If the chief district judge for your district prefers not to deal with the fugitive at this point, your release is on condition that the person either (a) return for a district court appearance at a specific time within thirty days or (b) surrender when a governor's warrant is issued. If the governor's warrant has not been issued by the time of that first district court appearance, the district judge can continue the case for additional thirty-day periods up to a total of ninety days.

(*Note*: A law enforcement officer may re-arrest a fugitive on a new fugitive warrant based on the same charge. The officer should exercise discretion when re-arresting a suspected fugitive before the issuance of a governor's warrant. The officer should contact the demanding jurisdiction and affirmatively determine that it still wants the fugitive, will in fact seek the fugitive's return, and will timely process and forward the required documents to support the issuance of a governor's warrant.)

If the Officer Arrested the Fugitive on the Basis of a Warrant and Is Now Bringing the Fugitive before You

Inform the fugitive of the charges. The procedure is the same as if the person were charged with a North Carolina crime. The person should be informed of the charge against him or her, the right to communicate with counsel and friends, and whether he or she is entitled to bail.

Determine whether to allow bail. G.S. 15A-736 allows bail for a fugitive unless the offense with which he or she is charged in the other state is punishable by death or life imprisonment. Apparently the only form of pretrial release that may be used is a bail bond with sureties. The bail bond schedule given the magistrate by the senior resident superior court judge may include instructions on what bond to set for fugitives. Sometimes the same amount is required as for a similar North Carolina crime, and sometimes the amount is doubled or otherwise multiplied. If bail is not allowed, or if the defendant cannot meet the bail, he or she should be committed to the county jail.

(*Note*: Bail is not allowed (1) after a governor's warrant has been issued, (2) the fugitive had previously executed a pre-signed waiver of extradition, typically as a probationer, parolee, or post-release supervisee, or (3) the person was transferred from another state to North Carolina under the Interstate Compact for Adult Offender Supervision (see pages 4–5) for supervision as a parolee, post-release supervisee, or probationer, and the state under the compact seeks to retake the person and the person has been arrested or detained under the compact's procedures. A person taken into custody under the Interstate Compact for Adult Offender Supervision is not returned to a state under the extradition process, but the no-bail issue is mentioned here so magistrates have this information if such a person appears before them.)

Order the fugitive to appear in district court. Whether the fugitive is released on bond or cannot make bond or is ineligible for bail, the release or commitment order should direct that he or she appear before a district court judge at the earliest possible session of court. Although the statute does not require an immediate district court appearance for the fugitive who is released on bond, such an appearance will give the district judge an early opportunity to review the fugitive's bond, explain the extradition process, and appoint counsel if necessary. Fugitives often waive formal extradition once they are told about the process and have talked to a lawyer. If the chief district judge for your district prefers not to deal with the fugitive at this point, your release is on condition that the fugitive either return for a district court appearance at a specific time within thirty days or surrender when a governor's warrant is issued. If the governor's warrant has not been issued by the time of that first district court appearance, the district judge can continue the case for additional thirty-day periods up to a total of ninety days.

(*Note*: A law enforcement officer may re-arrest a fugitive on a new fugitive warrant based on the same charge. The officer should exercise discretion when re-arresting a suspected fugitive before the issuance of a governor's warrant. The officer should contact the demanding jurisdiction and affirmatively determine that it still wants the fugitive, will in fact seek the fugitive's return, and will timely process and forward the required documents to support the issuance of a governor's warrant.)

If the Fugitive Has Been Arrested on a Governor's Warrant

Inform the fugitive of the charges. Tell the fugitive what crime he or she is charged with in the other state (the fugitive was also given this information when first arrested in North Carolina) and that the Governor of North Carolina has issued a warrant for him or her to be taken into custody and returned to the state from which the fugitive fled. Also inform the fugitive of the right to communicate with counsel and friends. The governor's warrant requires that the fugitive be held without bond. The governor's warrant is an original warrant of arrest and supersedes the fugitive warrant.

Commit the fugitive to jail. Commit the fugitive to jail to await his or her appearance before a district court judge.

Order the fugitive returned to district court at the earliest possible court session. The order of commitment should specify the time and date that the fugitive is to appear before a district court judge, which should be as early as possible. At that time he or she will be informed of the right to apply for a writ of habeas corpus.

When the Fugitive Has Not Yet Been Charged with a Crime in the Other State

The extradition statutes also allow a fugitive to be arrested in North Carolina even though he or she has not yet been formally charged in the other state. This situation rarely occurs. It is most likely to happen when the person commits a crime in a neighboring state and immediately flees to North Carolina, where local law enforcement officers are asked to arrest the person before officers in the other state have found a judicial official to issue an arrest warrant there. Before a North Carolina officer may make an arrest in this situation, he or she must obtain an arrest warrant. The procedure you follow in issuing such a warrant is the same one used when the officer wants to charge someone with a North Carolina crime. That is, the officer must be placed under oath and must state facts from which you can independently determine whether there is probable cause to believe the person committed the crime in another state.

You cannot simply accept the word of the officers from the other state that the person committed the crime; you must be told the reasons for reaching that conclusion. (This is different from other situations involving a fugitive, when you need only establish that the person has been charged in the other state and may not inquire about the probable cause for that charge.) If you determine that there is probable cause, complete an arrest warrant. The standard arrest warrant form will need to be modified to indicate that the crime is one committed against the law of another state. You need not spell out the elements of the offense but can simply state the name of the crime in the other state. Use the name of the crime given by the officers from that state, which may be different from the name used in North Carolina (for example, "second-degree robbery"). After the warrant is issued, the case proceeds like any other involving a fugitive.

Duties of the Clerk of Court
When the Fugitive Is First Arrested

The district court hearing. When the fugitive is arrested, he or she will be taken to a magistrate, just like anyone else arrested in North Carolina, and will either be committed to jail or given pretrial release. In either case, the magistrate should have scheduled the person to appear in district court as soon as possible. Although a fugitive released on bail need not be immediately scheduled for a district court appearance—he or she could simply be released on bond on condition that the fugitive return at the end of thirty days or whenever a governor's warrant is issued—the magistrate has been advised in this manual to set a district court appearance for the fugitive at the earliest possible session. An early appearance gives the judge an opportunity to explain the extradition process and to determine whether the fugitive needs an attorney, which may well result in an early waiver of the formal extradition procedures.

The clerk normally will have no responsibility regarding the setting of the fugitive's appearance before the judge other than placing the hearing on the calendar for the date set by the magistrate. However, there is one possible, though rare, exception. A clerk could conduct an appearance for a fugitive who is arrested on a governor's warrant for which there is no pending extradition proceeding (for example, a fugitive warrant was dismissed by a judge and then the governor issued a warrant for arrest) and no magistrate or judge is available. In such a case, the clerk must commit the fugitive to a detention facility with no bail allowed. If the fugitive is indigent and requests counsel during the appearance before the clerk, the clerk could appoint counsel and set the date for the fugitive's appearance before a judge. However, in counties with a public defender's office, an attorney for an indigent fugitive may be provided through that office.

If the Fugitive Waives Extradition in District Court

While the fugitive is in district court, he or she may decide to waive extradition. A judge will handle the waiver if court is in session, while the clerk or assistant clerk will do so at other times. Use AOC-CR-912M (available through the N.C. Court System website[11]). Whoever accepts the waiver

---

11. AOC-CR-912M is available at www.nccourts.org/Forms/Documents/171.pdf.

should explain the fugitive's rights to him or her. (*Note*: A magistrate is not authorized to take a waiver.)

A fugitive who waives extradition is not entitled to bond. G.S. 15A-746 states that the "judge or clerk of superior court shall direct the officer having such person in custody to deliver forthwith such person to the duly accredited agent or agents of the demanding state." The agents of the other state will not be allowed to come to North Carolina to return the fugitive to the other state if they are not guaranteed that the fugitive is in custody.

The clerk is responsible for seeing that the papers are handled correctly. One copy of the waiver goes in the case file, one copy goes to the extradition secretary on behalf of the governor, and one copy goes to the jail with the fugitive (to be given to the officer from the other state when he or she takes custody). Generally the clerk is to determine that copies of all correspondence involving the fugitive are kept in the case file. The sheriff is responsible for notifying the officers in the other state that the fugitive is ready to be returned.

If the Fugitive Refuses to Waive Extradition

If the fugitive does not waive extradition during his or her appearance in district court, and is indigent, the district court judge usually will appoint an attorney to represent the fugitive. However, in counties with a public defender's office, an attorney for an indigent fugitive may be provided through that office. Although the statutes do not require appointment of counsel until later in the process, matters can be expedited if the fugitive has an attorney. The attorney should be provided with a copy of the appointment, the warrant, and a notice of the next court date.

G.S. 15A-601, which among its provisions sometimes requires a clerk in a criminal proceeding to conduct a first appearance that often involves the appointment of an attorney, is inapplicable to the extradition process because extradition is not a criminal charge as described in the statute. Although rare, a clerk can appoint counsel for an indigent fugitive if the request for counsel occurs outside a session of court. But even when a clerk appoints counsel, he or she cannot exercise other authority given to judges in extradition proceedings. For example, the clerk could not extend the extradition hearing date beyond the original thirty days from arrest to allow more time for the issuance and service of the governor's warrant because an extension can be granted only by a judge (or magistrate, but a magistrate would likely never exercise that authority).

It is likely that at the fugitive's appearance in district court the judge will continue the case for thirty days. The defendant will be ordered to return on a given date to see whether the Governor of North Carolina has issued a governor's warrant to have the fugitive returned to the other state. If the governor's warrant is issued before thirty days, a fugitive who is out on bail should be returned to custody and taken immediately before a district court judge. If no governor's warrant is issued and the fugitive returns as scheduled in thirty days, the case can be continued and another appearance scheduled later.

The statute allows the judge to continue the fugitive's bond or commitment for sixty additional days if the governor's warrant has not been issued by the end of the first thirty-day period, but judges usually continue a case for two additional thirty-day periods rather than one sixty-day period. The judge will decide whether the fugitive is to be given bond during this time. The clerk's responsibility is to record the information on the commitment paper or release order. If the other state shows no urgency in carrying out formal extradition, the judge may simply release the fugitive after sixty days—not waiting the full ninety days. If the judge releases the fugitive because no governor's warrant has been issued, the clerk closes the case as a dismissal. The dismissal of the fugitive warrant does not permanently bar the state's attempt to extradite the fugitive. A governor's warrant may be issued and served after the dismissal of the fugitive warrant, and a district court hearing will be set and proceed as if the fugitive warrant never existed.

Prepare copies of the governor's warrant. In most cases when a governor's warrant is issued, the original and one copy are sent to the clerk's office for delivery to the sheriff's office. Sometimes they are sent directly to the sheriff's office or to the district attorney's office for delivery to the sheriff, with the original to be sent to the clerk's office. The clerk should notify the sheriff that the warrant has been received and should make another copy for the fugitive. In addition to the fugitive's copy, the original governor's warrant and one other copy are sent to the jail to be signed by the officers from the other state when they come. If the fugitive is not still in custody, the governor's warrant is given to an officer to bring the fugitive back into custody. The fugitive should be scheduled for the next session of district court.

In district court the judge will tell the fugitive that he or she may apply for a writ of habeas corpus, will make sure an indigent fugitive gets a lawyer if he or she does not already have one, and will give the fugitive a certain amount of time (though still in custody) to decide whether to apply for a writ of habeas corpus—ten days is usually sufficient to file a petition. The case is then continued for the period set by the district judge. If the fugitive does not apply for a writ of habeas corpus by the set time, the district judge orders him or her turned over to the agents from the other state. If the fugitive does apply for a writ of habeas corpus, the case becomes a pending case in superior court to be set for a hearing by a superior court judge.

Place a copy of the governor's warrant in the file and return the original to the attorney general's office in care of the extradition secretary. Once the fugitive is turned over to the agents from the other state—either with or without a habeas corpus hearing in superior court—the original governor's warrant is returned to the attorney general's office, care of the extradition secretary, and one copy is placed in the court record. (*Note:* It is important that the final disposition of the case is noted on the governor's warrant being returned to the extradition secretary.)

Duties of the Prosecutor
When the Fugitive Is First Arrested

When first arrested, the fugitive may be given bond by a magistrate, unless the crime is one punishable by death or life imprisonment or the fugitive is a probationer, parolee, or post-release supervisee who had executed a pre-signed waiver of extradition. Whether the fugitive is held or released on bond, the magistrate should schedule him or her for the next session of district court. If the fugitive is released on bail, the immediate appearance in district court is not required by the statute—the magistrate could schedule the district court appearance thirty days later—but an immediate appearance will usually expedite matters. At the district court appearance the judge should inform the fugitive of the charge against him or her, make sure that the fugitive has a copy of the arrest warrant or magistrate's order, review the bail, and determine whether it is necessary to appoint an attorney. In counties with a public defender's office, an attorney for an indigent fugitive may be provided through that office. The fugitive may waive extradition and be turned over to an agent from the other state, or he or she may be continued on bonded release or in commitment for up to thirty days (from the time of the initial arrest in North Carolina) to await issuance of a governor's warrant.

When the Fugitive Appears in District Court at the End of Thirty Days

If the recommended procedure has been followed, the fugitive will have already appeared before a district judge once, when first arrested, though he or she could have been released by a magistrate for thirty days without having seen a judge. In either case, the only purpose of this district court appearance is to determine whether the Governor of North Carolina has issued a governor's warrant ordering the fugitive's return to the other state. Before the hearing, the prosecutor should determine whether the governor's warrant has been issued. If the warrant has been issued, the prosecutor should proceed as indicated below. If not, the fugitive may be held or released on bond for another sixty days to await issuance of the governor's warrant. Judges usually continue the case for thirty days at a time. Before the prosecutor asks for another thirty-day commitment, he or she should try to determine whether the other state is diligently pursuing extradition.

When a Governor's Warrant Is Issued

When a governor's warrant is issued, the fugitive is to be taken into custody (the fugitive may already be in custody if he or she was denied bail or could not make bail) and brought before a district court judge. The judge is to inform the fugitive of the other state's demand for his or her surrender, the charged crime, the entitlement to counsel if indigent, and that he or she has a reasonable time, set by the judge, within which to apply for a writ of habeas corpus. Because the grounds that can be raised are very limited, ten days is usually sufficient time to file a petition. The fugitive may not be turned over to the agent of the other state until this appearance has been held, unless the fugitive decides to waive extradition. Bail is not allowed once a governor's warrant has been issued.

When the Fugitive Applies for a Writ of Habeas Corpus

The prosecutor is to be notified if the fugitive applies for a writ of habeas corpus and will represent the state of North Carolina at that hearing. As discussed in the section of this manual titled "Legal Issues in Extradition," the issues that may be raised at the habeas corpus hearing are limited to the following:

Whether the demand for extradition was made in the proper form. G.S. 15A-723 requires that the demand for extradition include a copy of the indictment, information, or warrant plus supporting affidavits used to charge the defendant in the other state. If the fugitive is an escapee, the other state must send a copy of the judgment of conviction or the sentence imposed with a statement that the person has escaped or has broken the terms of bail, probation, parole, or post-release supervision. The indictment, information, or warrant and affidavit must substantially charge the person with a crime in the other state and must be authenticated by the governor of that state. Minor defects in the wording of the charge from the other state do not invalidate a charge, nor is there any particular form required for the authentication by the governor.

Identity of the fugitive. The defendant has the burden of showing that he or she is not the fugitive being sought. Identification is facilitated when photographs, fingerprints, or an identification page accompany the extradition papers. Sometimes an identifying witness must be brought from the other state. A determination that the defendant is not the fugitive being sought does not prevent a later extradition proceeding against the same person for a similar charge.

Whether the person is a fugitive from the other state. The recital in the governor's warrant that the defendant is a fugitive from the other state creates a presumption that he or she is, placing the burden on the defendant to show otherwise. If the charge is one that required his or her presence in the other state, the fugitive can meet the burden by showing that he or she was not there when the crime was committed. The reason for leaving the other state is irrelevant. The demand from the other state may omit a statement that the defendant was present when the crime was committed, if the nature of the crime is such that his or her presence is implicit in the commission.

Extradition of a person who commits acts in another state intentionally resulting in a crime in the charging state is allowed. The charging state's requisition and supporting documents should clearly state whether the accused is a fugitive or the request is for a non-fugitive. (*Note:* A non-fugitive extradition is discretionary with the governor, not mandatory.)

Whether the defendant has been charged with a crime. The defendant may show, by introducing the relevant statutes, that his or her acts do not amount to a crime in the other state.

The governor's warrant is presumed valid, and the burden is on the defendant to disprove its allegations. Unless the matter is related to one of the issues above, it is not relevant to consider the defendant's guilt or innocence, an alibi, the other state's motive in extraditing, the expiration of the statute of limitations, or any constitutional matter, such as whether the defendant is likely to receive a fair trial or the quality of prison conditions in the other state.

A judgment denying a writ of habeas corpus is a final judgment of the superior court for which the defendant may seek certiorari to the North Carolina Court of Appeals. The state may seek certiorari to review a judgment granting a writ of habeas corpus. The superior court judge or a court of appeals judge may issue a stay to allow the court of appeals to hear the defendant's appeal.

If the Fugitive Is Also Charged with a Crime in North Carolina

G.S. 15A-739 allows the Governor of North Carolina to delay extradition if the person being sought by the other state has been charged with a crime in North Carolina. The extradition secretary should be notified that a North Carolina charge is pending before the governor's warrant is issued.

Duties of the District Court Judge
When the Fugitive Is First Arrested

Normally a district court judge will have no involvement in the initial arrest of a fugitive. The judge could be called on to issue an arrest warrant just as a magistrate would, but that should rarely happen.

Appearance before a District Court Judge

G.S. 15A-601, the statute requiring a first appearance before a district court judge, refers to crimes "in the original jurisdiction of the superior court." Because the fugitive is charged with a crime in another state, it is not required under that statute that a first appearance he held, but magistrates are advised to schedule all fugitives, whether committed or released on bail, to appear at the next session of district court. This procedure can expedite matters considerably. At the appearance the judge should advise the fugitive of the charge against him or her, make sure the fugitive has a copy of the arrest warrant or magistrate's order, and review the bail set by the magistrate. The fugitive may waive extradition at this appearance (see the section in this manual titled "If the Fugitive Wishes to Waive Extradition").

If the fugitive cannot make bail or if he or she is denied bail, the fugitive should be committed to jail to be returned to district court on a specific date within thirty days of arrest. At that time there will be a determination whether a governor's warrant has been issued. If he or she is released on bond after the appearance in court, the release should be conditioned on a return to district court on a specific date within thirty days to determine whether the governor's warrant has been issued or to return whenever the warrant is issued if it is sooner than thirty days.

Usually the appearance is used to determine whether counsel should be appointed if the fugitive is indigent. Although the extradition statutes, in particular G.S. 15A-730, provide for the fugitive to be notified of the right to counsel after the governor's warrant has been issued (when the fugitive is returned to custody and taken before a judge to be informed of the right to apply for a writ of habeas corpus), the need for counsel should be determined at the appearance. (In counties with a public defender's office, an attorney for an indigent fugitive may be provided through that office.) Doing so often helps in informing the defendant of the extradition process and in helping him or her decide whether to waive formal extradition.

When the Fugitive Returns to Court after Thirty Days

Whether the fugitive is out on bond or has been committed to jail, he or she is to return to district court within thirty days of his or her arrest in North Carolina. This appearance is used to determine whether the Governor of North Carolina has issued a governor's warrant ordering that the fugitive be returned to the other state. If the warrant has been issued, the judge should proceed as indicated in the next section.

If the governor's warrant has not been issued, the fugitive may be continued on bond or committed to jail for up to sixty additional days to await issuance of the governor's warrant. The usual practice is to continue the case for thirty days at a time. Before an additional thirty-day custody is imposed, the prosecutor or a law enforcement officer should be required to determine whether the other state is diligently pursuing extradition. Of course the fugitive may use this opportunity to waive extradition and return voluntarily to the other state.

When a Governor's Warrant Has Been Issued

Once a governor's warrant is issued, G.S. 15A-730 requires that the fugitive be brought before a judge before he or she is delivered to the agent of the other state. At the district court appearance after the arrest on a governor's warrant, the judge is to inform the fugitive of the other state's demand for his or her return, the charge against him or her in that state, that the fugitive has the right to demand and procure counsel, and that he or she may challenge the legality of the arrest by applying for a writ of habeas corpus. If the fugitive wants counsel and is indigent, the judge should appoint counsel if that has not already been done. (In counties with a public defender's office, an attorney for an indigent fugitive may be provided through that office.) The statute also requires that the fugitive be given a reasonable time within which to apply for a writ of habeas corpus. Because the grounds that can be raised are limited, ten days is usually sufficient time in which to file a petition. The time limit is to be fixed by the district court judge. The judge should order that the fugitive be held in the county jail or other place of confinement until the time expires for applying for a writ of habeas corpus; the person is then to be turned over to the agent for the other state. Once a governor's warrant is issued, bail is not allowed.

If the Fugitive Wishes to Waive Extradition

At any time after the fugitive has been arrested, he or she may waive extradition and be delivered to an agent from the other state. G.S. 15A-746 allows the waiver to be made before a judge or a clerk or assistant clerk of superior court. The waiver must be in writing; use AOC-CR-912M (available through the N.C. Court System website[12]). Before the form is signed, the fugitive must be told (a) that he or she may refuse to waive extradition and may require the other state to make a formal request for extradition and (b) that if a governor's warrant is issued he or she may apply for a writ of habeas corpus. When the waiver is signed, one copy is to be forwarded to the extradition secretary on behalf of the governor and one copy is to be given to the agent from the other state. The judge should order the fugitive released to that agent. If the agent is not present, the fugitive should be ordered held in jail until the agent arrives.

An agent should arrange to take custody of the fugitive at the earliest possible time following notification that the fugitive is ready to be surrendered. While federal law (18 U.S.C. § 3182) implies that a fugitive is to remain in custody at least thirty days to await the arrival of agents from the demanding state, local jurisdictions frequently require that the agents appear in a much shorter time. (*Note*: If the charging state has failed to take possession of the

---

12. AOC-CR-912M is available at www.nccourts.org/Forms/Documents/171.pdf.

fugitive within thirty days of documented notification, the fugitive should be allowed to apply for a writ of habeas corpus demanding his or her release.)

Duties of the Superior Court Judge
When the Fugitive Is First Arrested
The superior court judge should have no direct involvement in an extradition case unless the fugitive applies for a writ of habeas corpus. The senior resident superior court judge is to issue a bail policy to be used by the magistrates in his or her district, and that policy should indicate what bond is to be required of a fugitive. The extradition statute on bail, G.S. 15A-736, allows bail unless the offense is punishable by death or life imprisonment but only on a secured appearance bond. Once a governor's warrant is issued, bail is not allowed.

When the Fugitive Applies for a Writ of Habeas Corpus
After the governor's warrant is issued, a fugitive may apply for a writ of habeas corpus, and the superior court judge has the duty to schedule a hearing on the writ. As discussed in greater detail in the section of this manual titled "Legal Issues in Extradition," the issues that may be raised at the habeas corpus hearing are limited to the following:

Whether the demand for extradition has been made in the proper form. G.S. 15A-723 requires that the demand for extradition include a copy of the indictment, information, or warrant—with supporting affidavits—used to charge the defendant in the other state. If the fugitive is an escapee, the other state must send a copy of the judgment of conviction or the sentence imposed with a statement that the person has escaped or has broken the terms of his or her bail, probation, parole, or post-release supervision. The indictment, information, or warrant and supporting affidavit must substantially charge the person with a crime in the other state and must be authenticated by the governor of that state. Minor defects in the wording of the charge from the other state do not invalidate a charge, nor is there any particular form required for the authentication by the governor.

Identity of the fugitive. The defendant has the burden of showing that he or she is not the fugitive being sought. Identification can be facilitated by photographs, fingerprints, or an identification page accompanying the extradition papers. Sometimes an identifying witness must be brought from the other state. A determination that the defendant is not the fugitive being sought does not prevent a subsequent extradition proceeding against the same person for a similar charge.

Whether the person is a fugitive from the other state. The recital in the governor's warrant that the defendant is a fugitive from the other state creates a presumption that he or she is, and the burden is on the defendant to show otherwise. If the charge is one that required his or her presence in the other state, the fugitive can meet that burden by showing that he or she was not there when the crime was committed. The reason for leaving the other state is irrelevant. The demand from the other state may omit a statement that the defendant was present when the crime was committed, if the nature of the crime is such that his or her presence is implicit in the commission.

Extradition of people who commit acts while in another state intentionally resulting in a crime in the charging state is allowed. The charging state's requisition and supporting documents should clearly state whether the accused is a fugitive or the request is for a non-fugitive. (*Note*: A non-fugitive extradition is discretionary with the governor, not mandatory.)

Whether the defendant has been charged with a crime. The defendant may show, by introducing the relevant statutes, that his or her acts do not amount to a crime in the other state.

The governor's warrant is presumed valid, and the burden is on the defendant to disprove the allegations. Unless the matter is related to one of the issues above, it is not relevant to consider the defendant's guilt or innocence, an alibi, the other state's motive in extraditing, the expiration of the statute of limitations, or any constitutional matter such as whether the defendant is likely to receive a fair trial or the quality of prison conditions in the other state.

A judgment denying a writ of habeas corpus is a final judgment of the superior court for which the defendant may seek certiorari to the North Carolina Court of Appeals. The state may seek certiorari to review a judgment granting a writ of habeas corpus. The superior court judge or a court of appeals judge may issue a stay to allow the court of appeals to hear the defendant's appeal.

If the Fugitive Wishes to Waive Extradition

At any time after the fugitive has been arrested (included after a governor's warrant has been issued), he or she may waive extradition and be delivered to an agent from the other state. G.S. 15A-746 allows the waiver to be made before a judge or a clerk or assistant clerk of superior court. The waiver must be in writing; use AOC-CR-912M (available through the N.C. Court System website[13]). Before the form is signed, the fugitive must be told (a) that he or she may refuse to waive extradition and may require the other state to make a formal request for extradition and (b) that if a governor's warrant is issued, he or she may apply for a writ of habeas corpus. When the waiver is signed, one copy is to be forwarded to the extradition secretary on behalf of the governor and one copy is to be given to the agent from the other state. The judge should order the fugitive released to that agent. If the agent is not present, the fugitive should be ordered held in jail until the agent arrives.

An agent should arrange to take custody of the fugitive at the earliest possible time following notification that the fugitive is ready to be surrendered. While federal law (18 U.S.C. § 3182) implies that a fugitive is to remain in custody at least thirty days to await the arrival of agents from the demanding state, local jurisdictions frequently require that the agents appear in a much shorter time. (*Note*: If the charging state has failed to take possession of the fugitive within thirty days of documented notification, the fugitive should be allowed to apply for a writ of habeas corpus demanding his or her release.)

---

13. AOC-CR-912M is available at www.nccourts.org/Forms/Documents/171.pdf.

Legal Issues in Extradition

What issues may a governor consider in deciding whether extradition is proper in a given case?

The United States Supreme Court has ruled that a governor has a mandatory duty to comply with a proper demand for a fugitive, and a federal court has the authority to compel the governor to perform this duty. Puerto Rico v. Branstad, 483 U.S. 219 (1987). A governor may only consider the following issues when deciding whether extradition is proper: (1) whether the extradition documents on their face are in order, (2) whether the accused has been charged with a crime in the demanding state, (3) whether the accused is the person named in the request for extradition, and (4) whether the accused is a fugitive. Michigan v. Doran, 439 U.S. 282 (1978); California v. Super. Ct. of Cal., 482 U.S. 400 (1987); New Mexico v. Reed, 524 U.S. 151 (1998) (allegation that extraditing state will deny fugitive due process and fugitive would be physically harmed in prison are not issues that may be raised in extradition hearing); State of Alabama v. Engler, 85 F.3d 1205 (6th Cir. 1996).

What is the meaning of "fugitive from justice"?

The term "fugitive from justice" is broadly defined as a person who commits a crime in a state and then leaves its jurisdiction. It is unnecessary to show that the person was charged before leaving the state or that the person fled to avoid prosecution. A person is a fugitive even if he or she left the state with the state's consent. *See* 31A AM. JUR. 2D *Extradition* § 23 (2012); *In re*

Sultan, 115 N.C. 57 (1894); Gee v. Kansas, 912 F.2d 414 (10th Cir. 1990) (even if fugitive leaves state with knowledge and consent of state officials, his or her fugitive status is unaffected); Dunn v. Hindman, 836 F. Supp. 750 (D. Kan. 1993).

Is the fugitive entitled to be released on bail before the governor's warrant is issued?

G.S. 15A-736 states that the magistrate or judge "may admit the person arrested to bail by bond" unless the person is charged with a crime punishable by death or life imprisonment under the laws of the state in which it was committed. The statute mentions release only by bail with sufficient sureties.

Is the fugitive entitled to a hearing before a governor's warrant can be issued?

The general rule is that he or she is not entitled to a hearing. Application of Dugger, 497 P.2d 413 (Ariz. Ct. App. 1972); Home v. Wilson, 306 F. Supp. 753 (E.D. Tenn. 1969); Scheinfain v. Aldredge, 12 S.E.2d 868 (Ga. 1941).

Must a fugitive be released if the governor's warrant has not been issued by the time the fugitive has been committed for the maximum period, a total of ninety days as permitted under G.S. 15A-735 (up to thirty days) and G.S. 15A-737 (extension permitted up to sixty days)?

Yes. Brightman v. Withrow, 304 S.E.2d 688 (W. Va. 1983) (but fugitive remains subject to re-arrest under governor's warrant); Speaks v. McGregor, 355 F. Supp. 1129 (W.D. Va. 1973); People *ex rel.* Linaris v. Weizenecker, 392 N.Y.S.2d 813 (Putnam Cnty. Ct. 1977).

If a fugitive is released because a governor's warrant has not been issued within ninety days under G.S. 15A-735 and G.S. 15A-737, may a new fugitive warrant be issued?

Yes. The dismissal of the first fugitive warrant is not a bar to a second fugitive warrant under the Double Jeopardy Clause because that clause applies only to trials. *Cf.* Collins v. Loisel, 262 U.S. 426 (1923). Nor is there a statutory bar to the issuance of a second fugitive warrant.

May a fugitive be re-arrested with a governor's warrant after a fugitive warrant has been dismissed?

Yes. Debski v. New Hampshire, 348 A.2d 343 (N.H. 1975); Brightman v. Withrow, 304 S.E.2d 688 (W. Va. 1983); Commonwealth *ex rel.* Douglass v. Aytch, 310 A.2d 313 (Pa. Super. Ct. 1973).

May a second governor's warrant be issued after the first governor's warrant was dismissed because of technical errors?

Yes. Cain v. Moore, 438 A.2d 723 (Conn. 1980).

Does a person held for extradition have a right to be released on bail after a governor's warrant has been issued?

The majority rule is that the Uniform Extradition Law does *not* grant a right to bail to a person being held for extradition after a governor's warrant is issued. Emig v. Hayward, 703 P.2d 1043 (Utah 1985); *In re* Iverson, 376 A.2d 23 (Vt. 1977); *In re* Ford, 468 N.W.2d 260 (Mich. Ct. App. 1991); People v. Super. Ct. (*Ruiz*), 234 Cal. Rptr. 214 (Cal. Ct. App. 1986); Balasco v. State, 289 So. 2d 666 (Ala. Crim. App. 1974); State *ex rel.* Howard v. St. Joseph Super. Ct., 316 N.E.2d 356 (Ind. 1974). Most courts have also ruled that judges have no common law or inherent power to grant release on bail in such circumstances. See the cases cited above and Carol Crocca, *Right of Extraditee to Bail after Issuance of Governor's Warrant and Pending Final Disposition of Habeas Corpus Claim*, 13 A.L.R. 5th 118 (1993). But also see *Carino v. Watson*, 370 A.2d 950 (Conn. 1976), which ruled that releasing a fugitive on bail was proper, even after a governor's warrant had been served on the fugitive; the opinion was based on the court's common law power to allow bail "in all cases"; *In re* Basto, 531 A.2d 355 (N.J. 1987) (allowing bail for fugitive who was not in demanding state when crime was committed).

The Office of the Governor agrees with the National Association of Extradition Officials' resolution in 1986 opposing bail in all cases when a governor's warrant has been issued. It takes the position that the governor's warrant is an executive—not judicial—warrant and that bail is not allowed.

Is a fugitive entitled to counsel at a habeas corpus hearing to contest the legality of an extradition proceeding?

Yes. Under G.S. 15A-730, an accused is entitled to have counsel present at such hearings. G.S. 7A-451(a)(5) provides that an indigent person is entitled to appointed counsel at an extradition hearing. Appointed counsel is not required at an initial arraignment on a fugitive warrant. Rutledge v. Preadmore, 176 N.W.2d 417 (Mich. Ct. App. 1970).

Most courts have ruled that counsel in such cases is required solely by statute and is not constitutionally required under the Sixth Amendment. McGuigan v. Sheriff, Wahoe Cnty., 669 F. Supp. 1037 (D. Nev. 1987); Wertheimer v. State, 201 N.W.2d 383 (Minn. 1972); Roberts v. Hocker, 456 P.2d 425 (Nev. 1969).

On what grounds may a fugitive challenge a governor's warrant in a habeas corpus proceeding?

The United States Supreme Court has ruled that a court may only consider the following issues when deciding whether extradition is proper: (1) whether the extradition documents on their face are in order, (2) whether the accused has been charged with a crime in the demanding state, (3) whether the accused is the person named in the request for extradition, and (4) whether the accused is a fugitive. California v. Super. Ct. of Cal., 482 U.S. 400 (1987). *See also* Michigan v. Doran, 439 U.S. 282 (1978); New Mexico v. Reed, 524 U.S. 151 (1998) (allegation that extraditing state will deny fugitive due process and fugitive would be physically harmed in prison are not issues that may be raised in extradition hearing); Dodd v. State, 56 N.C. App. 214 (1982); *In re* Armstrong, 49 N.C. App. 175 (1980). The defendant's evidence must be conclusive; mere conflicting testimony as to an accused's absence from the demanding state at the time of the alleged crime will not support his or her release from custody at a habeas corpus proceeding. People *ex rel.* Garner v. Clutts, 170 N.E.2d 538 (Ill. 1970); State *ex rel.* Zack v. Kriss 74 A.2d 25 (Md. 1952).

What is the standard of proof required for a fugitive who is challenging a governor's warrant in a habeas corpus proceeding? Does a state have the burden of producing evidence if a defendant introduces evidence contesting his or her status as a fugitive?

A governor's warrant creates a presumption of regularity in an extradition proceeding, and a fugitive who wishes to challenge the warrant must show by clear and convincing evidence that the warrant is invalid. People *ex rel.* Harris v. Warden, 345 N.Y.S.2d 29 (App. Div. 1973); Stolz v. Miller, 543 P.2d 513 (Colo. 1975); McCollough v. Darr, 548 P.2d 1245 (Kan. 1976). Other cases have formulated the standard of proof as requiring "conclusive" evidence, People *ex rel.* Pirone v. Police Comm'r, 225 N.Y.S.2d 257 (App. Div. 1962); or as requiring "clear and satisfactory" evidence, State *ex rel.* Rhodes v. Omodt, 218 N.W.2d 461 (Minn. 1974). In *Dodd v. State*, 56 N.C. App. 214 (1982), the North Carolina Court of Appeals ruled that the fugitive must prove beyond a reasonable doubt that he or she is not the person named in the extradition papers.

States differ on whether the prosecution must present evidence to rebut an alleged fugitive's evidence. In *Rhodes*, the court ruled that the state must present "minimal" evidence rebutting an alleged fugitive's evidence that he or she was not in the demanding state at the time of the crime. In *Stolz*, the court ruled that a statement by an alleged fugitive does not necessarily rebut the presumption of regularity created by the governor's warrant.

Must an indictment, information, or warrant from the demanding state be accompanied by affidavits or other documents showing the basis for the probable cause to arrest the fugitive?

An indictment is a sufficient finding of probable cause so that an asylum state may not look behind the documents to determine whether probable cause exists. U.S. *ex rel.* Davis v. Behagen, 436 F.2d 596 (2d Cir. 1970); People v. Jackson, 502 P.2d 1106 (Colo. 1972).

If the documents sent by the demanding state do not include an indictment, they must show that a detached and neutral judicial official in the demanding state has found probable cause. It is not required that an affidavit supporting probable cause must have been executed before the issuance of an arrest warrant. Dunn v. Hindman, 836 F. Supp. 750 (D. Kan. 1993).

If the governor in the asylum state decides to issue a governor's warrant, the courts of that state may not review the documents to see whether they contain a showing or probable cause. Michigan v. Doran, 439 U.S. 282 (1978); California v. Super. Ct. of Cal., 482 U.S. 400 (1987).

Does res judicata bar a state from proving in a second extradition hearing that the defendant was in the demanding state when the offense was committed if the state did not present sufficient evidence to prove that issue at the first extradition hearing?

Res judicata is not a bar to a second extradition hearing if new or additional evidence is presented at the second hearing. State *ex rel.* Moore v. Conrad, 371 S.E.2d 74 (W. Va. 1988); *In re* Russell, 524 P.2d 1295 (Cal. 1974); People *ex rel.* Schank v. Gerace, 661 N.Y.S.2d 403 (App. Div. 1997). *But see* Wells v. Sheriff, Carter Cnty., 442 P.2d 535 (Okla. Crim. App. 1968).

Are waivers of extradition by probationers and parolees that are executed as a condition of probation, parole, and post-release supervision valid when a state later seeks to rely on the waivers in extraditing them?

Yes. Goode v. Nobles, 518 S.E.2d 122 (Ga. 1999); Tymenski v. State, 816 So. 2d 814 (Fla. Dist. Ct. App. 2002); Pierson v. Grant, 527 F.2d 161 (8th Cir. 1975); Commonwealth v. Green, 581 A.2d 544 (Pa. 1990) (citing cases from other jurisdictions); State v. Lingle, 308 N.W.2d 531 (Neb. 1981). These waivers are commonly known as pre-signed waivers of extradition.

(*Note*: Even though the return of a person under the Interstate Compact for Adult Offender Supervision (ICAOS) (discussed on pages 4–5), does not involve the extradition process, a person who seeks a transfer of supervision under the compact to another state is required to waive extradition from *any* state as a condition of the transfer.)

Is a district court a court of record so a district court judge may accept a written waiver of extradition under G.S. 15A-746?

Yes. *See generally* Bain v. Hunt, 10 N.C. 572 (1825) (court stated that district court is a court of record).

Interstate Agreement on Detainers

Sometimes a person who is wanted for prosecution is already in prison. A prosecutor may lodge a "detainer" against the prisoner by notifying the prison authorities that the person has pending charges and thus prevent release of the prisoner without giving notice to the prosecutor. Almost all states, including North Carolina, have joined the Interstate Agreement on Detainers, which establishes procedures for resolving pending charges against a prisoner early in his or her detention in another state. (The agreement only applies to pending charges. The extradition process must be used to return a prisoner who has violated probation, parole, or post-release supervision, unless he or she had executed a pre-signed waiver of extradition (discussed on page 4). This section briefly explains the detainer procedure. (*Note*: Sometimes an executive agreement between the governors of two states is utilized instead of this interstate agreement, as discussed on page 27.)

The Interstate Agreement on Detainers appears in G.S. 15A-761. The agreement allows both the prisoner and the prosecutor to request early resolution of charges outstanding against the prisoner. The prison officials who have custody of the prisoner are required to notify the prisoner of any detainers lodged against him or her. The prisoner may then request final disposition of the charges. When the prisoner makes such a request, the prison officials notify the prosecutor in the other state and offer him or her the opportunity to take custody of the prisoner. The prosecutor must try the case within 180 days after the prosecutor receives the prisoner's request.

A judge may grant a delay in the trial deadline for good cause if either the prisoner or his or her lawyer is present.

If detainers have been lodged for other charges from the same state, the prosecutors responsible for the other charges also are notified of the prisoner's request for final disposition. The prisoner's request is considered a request for disposition of all charges pending in that state. Failure to prosecute any of the charges pending against the prisoner in that state within the 180-day period, or the extended deadline, means dismissal of the charges with prejudice.

The prosecutor also can force an early trial. A prosecutor who has a charge against a prisoner in another state may request temporary custody for trial. The governor of the other state can refuse to grant that request, but if the governor agrees—or if he or she does not object within thirty days—the prisoner is turned over for prosecution. The trial must be held within 120 days after the prisoner is delivered—again with delays possible for good cause—or the charges must be dismissed with prejudice. All prosecutors in the state who have a detainer on the prisoner are notified that he or she is being returned for prosecution so that they may make their own requests for temporary custody.

After trial, the prisoner is returned to the state where he or she was serving his or her sentence. Once the prisoner completes the sentence in the state where he or she was originally in prison, the prisoner is given back to the other state to serve the sentence imposed there.

The Department of Public Safety employs an administrator for the Interstate Agreement on Detainers. The administrator can provide additional information about detainers and the forms to be used in the procedures described above (919-716-3160).

Interstate Compact for Adult Offender Supervision and Retaking of Offender without Utilizing Extradition

Under the Interstate Compact for Adult Offender Supervision (ICAOS), of which all states and the District of Columbia are members, a parolee, post-release supervisee, or probationer may seek a transfer of supervision to another state. If the request is approved, the person's presence in the other state is not as a fugitive from justice as set out in the extradition statutes (the typical ground for extradition) because the person is lawfully in the other state. However, if the person while being supervised in the other state violates a condition of supervision or otherwise commits an act that permits or requires the sending state to seek the person's return, the compact has its own procedures outside the extradition process to retake the person to the sending state. These procedures ordinarily do not involve court proceedings. Any necessary hearings are conducted by a state's compact administrator or designee—see, for example, North Carolina's procedures set out in G.S. 148-65.8. If the person is detained in the other state under the compact's procedures and brought before a judicial official, no bail is allowed pending a hearing conducted by the compact administrator or designee to determine if there is an appropriate basis for returning the person to the sending state. For detailed information on the compact, see www.interstatecompact.org and the bench book tab that is available on the left side of the webpage.

(*Note*: Even though the return of a person under the compact does not involve the extradition process, a person who seeks a transfer of supervision to another state is required to waive extradition from *any* state as a condition of the transfer.)

The compact administrator in the North Carolina Department of Public Safety can be contacted at 919-716-3160.

Return of Juveniles under Interstate Compact for Juveniles

The Interstate Compact for Juveniles (G.S. 7B-4000 through -4002) pro vides uniform procedures among almost all of the states in dealing with (1) juveniles who run away from another state and come to North Carolina, (2) juveniles who run away from North Carolina and go to another state, (3) juveniles from other states who commit delinquent acts in North Carolina and whose dispositions need to be supervised in the juveniles' home states, (4) juveniles from North Carolina who commit delinquent acts in other states and whose dispositions need to be supervised in North Carolina, (5) juveniles in North Carolina who are alleged to have committed delinquent acts in other states, and (6) juveniles in other states who are alleged to have committed delinquents acts in North Carolina.

The compact does not include specific procedures or directives for dealing with interstate issues involving delinquent juveniles. These are provided, instead, by rules and forms issued by the Interstate Commission for Juveniles. The rules, forms, a bench book, a directory of state contact information, and other information about the compact are available on the commission's website at www.juvenilecompact.org.

Juvenile court counselors should be familiar with the compact procedures and forms. In addition, the state's compact administrator in the Division of Juvenile Justice of the Department of Public Safety can provide guidance (919-733-3388).

Statutes

Article 37.
Uniform Criminal Extradition Act.

§ 15A–721. Definitions.

Where appearing in this Article the term "Governor" includes any person performing the functions of Governor by authority of the law of this State. The term "executive authority" includes the Governor, and any person performing the functions of governor in a state other than this State. The term "state," referring to a state other than this State, includes any other state or territory, organized or unorganized, of the United States of America. (1937, c. 273, s. 1; 1973, c. 1286, s. 16.)

§ 15A–722. Duty of Governor as to fugitives from justice of other states.

Subject to the provisions of this Article, the provisions of the Constitution of the United States controlling, and any and all acts of Congress enacted in pursuance thereof, it is the duty of the Governor of this State to have arrested and delivered up to the executive authority of any other state of the United States any person charged in that state with treason, felony or other crime, who has fled from justice and is found in this State. (1937, c. 273, s. 2; 1973, c. 1286, s. 16.)

§ 15A–723. Form of demand for extradition.

No demand for the extradition of a person charged with crime in another state shall be recognized by the Governor unless in writing alleging, except in cases arising under G.S. 15A-726, that the accused was present in the demanding state at the time of the commission of the alleged crime, and that thereafter he fled from the state, and accompanied by a copy of an indictment found or by information supported by affidavit in the state having jurisdiction of the crime, or by a copy of an affidavit made before a magistrate there, together with a copy of any warrant which was issued thereupon; or by a copy of a judgment of conviction or of a sentence imposed in execution thereof, together with a statement by the executive authority of the demanding state that the person claimed has escaped from confinement or has broken the terms of his bail, probation or parole. The indictment, information, or affidavit made before the magistrate must substantially charge the person demanded with having committed a crime under the law of that state; and the copy of indictment, information, affidavit, judgment of conviction or sentence must be authenticated by the executive authority making the demand. (1937, c. 273, s. 3; 1973, c. 1286, s. 16.)

§ 15A–724. Governor may cause investigation to be made.

When a demand shall be made upon the Governor of this State by the executive authority of another state for the surrender of a person so charged with crime, the Governor may call upon the Attorney General or any prosecuting officer in this State to investigate or assist in investigating the demand, and to report to him the situation and circumstances of the person so demanded, and whether he ought to be surrendered. (1937, c. 273, s. 4; 1973, c. 1286, s. 16.)

§ 15A–725. Extradition of persons imprisoned or awaiting trial in another state or who have left the demanding state under compulsion.

When it is desired to have returned to this State a person charged in this State with a crime, and such person is imprisoned or is held under criminal proceedings then pending against him in another state, the Governor of this State may agree with the executive authority of such other state for the extradition of such person before the conclusion of such proceedings or his term of sentence in such other state, upon condition that such person be returned to such other state at the expense of this State as soon as the prosecution in this State is terminated.

The Governor of this State may also surrender on demand of the executive authority of any other state any person in this State who is charged in the manner provided in G.S. 15A-743 with having violated the laws of the state whose executive authority is making the demand, even though such person left the demanding state involuntarily. (1937, c. 273, s. 5; 1973, c. 1286, s. 16.)

§ 15A–726. Extradition of persons not present in demanding state at time of commission of crime.

The Governor of this State may also surrender, on demand of the executive authority of any other state, any person in this State charged in such other state in the manner provided in G.S. 15A-723 with committing an act in this State, or in a third state, intentionally resulting in a crime in the state whose executive authority is making the demand, and the provisions of this Article, not otherwise inconsistent, shall apply to such cases, even though the accused was not in that state at the time of the commission of the crime, and has not fled therefrom. (1937, c. 273, s. 6; 1973, c. 1286, s. 16.)

§ 15A–727. Issue of Governor's warrant of arrest; its recitals.

If the Governor decides that the demand should be complied with, he shall sign a warrant of arrest, which shall be sealed with the State seal, and be directed to any peace officer or other person whom he may think fit to entrust with the execution thereof. The warrant must substantially recite the facts necessary to the validity of its issuance. (1937, c. 273, s. 7; 1973, c. 1286, s. 16.)

§ 15A–728. Manner and place of execution of warrant.

Such warrant shall authorize the peace officer or other person to whom directed to arrest the accused at any time and any place where he may be found within the State, and to command the aid of all peace officers or other persons in the execution of the warrant, and to deliver the accused, subject to the provisions of this Article, to the duly authorized agent of the demanding state. (1937, c. 273, s. 8; 1973, c. 1286, s. 16.)

§ 15A–729. Authority of arresting officer.

Every such peace officer or other person empowered to make the arrest shall have the same authority, in arresting the accused, to command assistance therein as peace officers have by law in the execution of any criminal process directed to them, with like penalties against those who refuse their assistance. (1937, c. 273, s. 9; 1973, c. 1286, s. 16.)

§ 15A–730. Rights of accused person; application for writ of habeas corpus.

No person arrested upon such warrant shall be delivered over to the agent whom the executive authority demanding him shall have appointed to receive him unless he shall first be taken forthwith before a judge of a court of record in this State, who shall inform him of the demand made for his surrender and of the crime with which he is charged, and that he has the right to demand and procure legal counsel; and if the prisoner or his counsel shall state that he or they desire to test the legality of his arrest, the judge of such court of record shall fix a reasonable time to be allowed him within which to apply for a writ of habeas corpus. When such writ is applied for, notice thereof, and of the time and place of hearing thereon, shall be given to the prosecuting officer of the county in which the arrest is made and in which the accused is in custody, and to the said agent of the demanding state. (1937, c. 273, s. 10; 1973, c. 1286, s. 16.)

§ 15A–731. Penalty for noncompliance with § 15A–730.

Any officer who shall deliver to the agent for extradition of the demanding state a person in his custody under the Governor's warrant, in willful disobedience to G.S. 15A-730, shall be guilty of a Class 2 misdemeanor. (1937, c. 273, s. 11; 1973, c. 1286, s. 16; 1993, c. 539, s. 302; 1994, Ex. Sess., c. 24, s. 14(c).)

§ 15A–732. Confinement in jail when necessary.

The officer or person executing the Governor's warrant of arrest, or the agent of the demanding state to whom the prisoner may have been delivered, may, when necessary, confine the prisoner in the jail of any county or city through which he may pass; and the keeper of such jail must receive and safely keep the prisoner until the officer or person having charge of him is ready to proceed on his route, such officer or person being chargeable with the expense of keeping.

The officer or agent of a demanding state to whom a prisoner may have been delivered following extradition proceedings in another state, or to whom a prisoner may have been delivered after waiving extradition in such other state, and who is passing through this State with such a prisoner for the purpose of immediately returning such prisoner to the demanding state may, when necessary, confine the prisoner in the jail of any county or city through which he may pass; and the keeper of such jail must receive and safely keep the prisoner until the officer or agent having charge of him is ready to proceed on his route, such officer or agent, however, being charge-able with the expense of keeping: Provided, however, that such officer or agent shall produce and show to the keeper of such jail satisfactory writ-ten evidence of the fact that he is actually transporting such prisoner to the demanding state after a requisition by the executive authority of such demanding state. Such prisoner shall not be entitled to demand a new req-uisition while in this State. (1937, c. 273, s. 12; 1973, c. 1286, s. 16.)

§ 15A–733. Arrest prior to requisition.

Whenever any person within this State shall be charged on the oath of any credible person before any judge or magistrate of this State with the com-mission of any crime in any other state and, except in cases arising under G.S. 15A-726, with having fled from justice, or with having been convicted of a crime in that state and having escaped from confinement, or having broken the terms of his bail, probation or parole, or whenever complaint shall have been made before any judge or magistrate in this State, setting forth on the affidavit of any credible person in another state that a crime has been committed in such other state, and that the accused has been charged in such state with the commission of the crime, and, except in cases arising under G.S. 15A-726, has fled from justice, or with having been convicted of a crime in that state and having escaped from confinement, or having broken the terms of his bail, probation or parole, and is believed to be in this State, the judge or magistrate shall issue a warrant directed to any peace officer commanding him to apprehend the person named therein, wherever he may be found in this State, and to bring him before the same or any other judge, magistrate or court who or which may be available in or convenient of access to the place where the arrest may be made, to answer the charge or complaint and affidavit, and a certified copy of the sworn charge or com-plaint and affidavit upon which the warrant is issued shall be attached to the warrant. (1937, c. 273, s. 13; 1973, c. 1286, s. 16.)

§ 15A–734. Arrest without a warrant.

The arrest of a person may be lawfully made also by any peace officer or a private person, without a warrant, upon reasonable information that the accused stands charged in the courts of a state with a crime punishable by death or imprisonment for a term exceeding one year, but when so arrested the accused must be taken before a judge or magistrate with all practicable speed, and complaint must be made against him under oath setting forth the ground for the arrest as in G.S. 15A-733; and thereafter his answer shall be heard as if he had been arrested on a warrant. (1937, c. 273, s. 14; 1973, c. 1286, s. 16.)

§ 15A–735. Commitment to await requisition; bail.

If from the examination before the judge or magistrate it appears that the person held is the person charged with having committed the crime alleged and, except in cases arising under G.S. 15A-726, that he has fled from justice, the judge or magistrate must, by a warrant reciting the accusation, commit him to the county jail for such a time, not exceeding 30 days and specified in the warrant, as will enable the arrest of the accused to be made under a warrant of the Governor on a requisition of the executive authority of the state having jurisdiction of the offense, unless the accused give bail as provided in G.S. 15A-736, or until he shall be legally discharged. (1937, c. 273, s. 15; 1973, c. 1286, s. 16.)

§ 15A–736. Bail in certain cases; conditions of bond.

Unless the offense with which the prisoner is charged is shown to be an offense punishable by death or life imprisonment under the laws of the state in which it was committed, a judge or magistrate in this State may admit the person arrested to bail by bond, with sufficient sureties, and in such sum as he deems proper, conditioned for his appearance before him at a time specified in such bond, and for his surrender, to be arrested upon the warrant of the Governor of this State. (1937, c. 273, s. 16; 1973, c. 1286, s. 16.)

§ 15A–736.1: Recodified as G.S. 15A-534.6 by Session Laws 2007-484, s. 4, effective August 30, 2007.

§ 15A–737. Extension of time of commitment; adjournment.

If the accused is not arrested under warrant of the Governor by the expiration of the time specified in the warrant or bond, a judge or magistrate may discharge him or may recommit him for a further period not to exceed 60 days, or a judge or magistrate may again take bail for his appearance and surrender, as provided in G.S. 15A-736, but within a period not to exceed 60 days after the date of such new bond. (1937, c. 273, s. 17; 1973, c. 1286, s. 16.)

§ 15A–738. Forfeiture of bail.

If the prisoner is admitted to bail and fails to appear and surrender himself according to the conditions of his bond, the judge, or magistrate by proper order, shall declare the bond forfeited and order his immediate arrest without warrant if he be within this State. Recovery may be had on such bond in the name of the State as in the case of other bonds given by the accused in criminal proceedings within this State. (1937, c. 273, s. 18; 1973, c. 1286, s. 16.)

§ 15A–739. Persons under criminal prosecution in this State at time of requisition.

If a criminal prosecution has been instituted against such person under the laws of this State and is still pending, the Governor, in his discretion, either may surrender him on demand of the executive authority of another state or hold him until he has been tried and discharged or convicted and punished in this State. (1937, c. 273, s. 19; 1973, c. 1286, s. 16.)

§ 15A–740. Guilt or innocence of accused, when inquired into.

The guilt or innocence of the accused as to the crime of which he is charged may not be inquired into by the Governor or in any proceeding after the demand for extradition accompanied by a charge of crime in legal form as above provided shall have been presented to the Governor, except as it may be involved in identifying the person held as the person charged with the crime. (1937, c. 273, s. 20; 1973, c. 1286, s. 16.)

§ 15A–741. Governor may recall warrant or issue alias.

The Governor may recall his warrant of arrest or may issue another warrant whenever he deems proper. (1937, c. 273, s. 21; 1973, c. 1286, s. 16.)

§ 15A–742. Fugitives from this State; duty of governors.

Whenever the Governor of this State shall demand a person charged with a crime or with escaping from confinement or breaking the terms of his bail, probation or parole in this State from the executive authority of any other state, or from the chief justice or an associate justice of the Supreme Court of the District of Columbia authorized to receive such demand under the laws of the United States, he shall issue a warrant under the seal of this State, to some agent, commanding him to receive the person so charged if delivered to him and convey him to the proper officer of the county in this State in which the offense was committed. (1937, c. 273, s. 22; 1973, c. 1286, s. 16.)

§ 15A–743. Application for issuance of requisition; by whom made; contents.

(a) When the return to this State of a person charged with crime in this State is required, the prosecuting attorney shall present to the Governor his written application for a requisition for the return of the person charged, in which application shall be stated the name of the person so charged, the crime charged against him, the approximate time, place and circumstances of its commission, the state in which he is believed to be, including the location of the accused therein, at the time the application is made and certifying that, in the opinion of the said prosecuting attorney, the ends of justice require the arrest and return of the accused to this State for trial and that the proceeding is not instituted to enforce a private claim.

(b) When the return to this State is required of a person who has been convicted of a crime in this State and has escaped from confinement or broken the terms of his bail, probation or parole, the prosecuting attorney of the county in which the offense was committed, the parole board, or the Director of Prisons or sheriff of the county from which escape was made, shall present to the Governor a written application for a requisition for the return of such person, in which application shall be stated the name of the person, the crime of which he was convicted, the circumstances of his escape from confinement or of the breach of the terms of his bail, probation or parole, the state in which he is believed to be, including the location of the person therein at the time application is made.

(c) The application shall be verified by affidavit, shall be executed in duplicate and shall be accompanied by two certified copies of the indictment returned, or information and affidavit filed, or of the complaint made to the judge or magistrate, stating the offense with which the accused is charged, or of the judgment of conviction or of the sentence. The prosecuting officer, parole board, warden or sheriff may also attach such further affidavits and other documents in duplicate as he shall deem proper to be submitted with such application. A copy of all papers shall be forwarded with the Governor's requisition. (1937, c. 273, s. 23; 1973, c. 1286, s. 16; 1975, c. 132; 1993, c. 83.)

§ 15A–744. Costs and expenses.

Subject to the requirements and restrictions set forth in this section, if the crime is a felony or if a person convicted in this State of a misdemeanor has broken the terms of his probation or parole, reimbursements for expenses shall be paid out of the State treasury on the certificate of the Governor. In all other cases, such expenses or reimbursements shall be paid out of the county treasury of the county wherein the crime is alleged to have been committed according to such regulations as the board of county commissioners may promulgate. In all cases, the expenses, for which repayment or reimbursement may be claimed, shall consist of the reasonable and necessary travel expense and subsistence costs of the extradition agent or fugitive officer, as well as the fugitive, together with such legal fees as were paid to the officials of the state on whose governor the requisition is made. The person or persons designated to return the fugitive shall not be allowed, paid or reimbursed for any expenses in connection with any requisition or extradition proceeding unless the expenses are itemized, the statement of same be sworn to under oath, and shall not then be paid or reimbursed unless a receipt is obtained showing the amount, the purpose for which said item or sum was expended, the place, date and to whom paid, and said receipt or receipts attached to said sworn statement and filed with the Governor. The Governor shall have the authority, upon investigation, to increase or decrease any item or expenses shown in said sworn statement, or to include items of expenses omitted by mistake or inadvertence. The decision or determination of the Governor as to the correct amount to be paid for such expenses or reimbursements shall be final. When it is deemed necessary for more than one agent, extradition agent, fugitive officer or person, to be designated to return a fugitive from another state to this State, the district attorney or prosecuting officer shall file with his written application to the Governor of this State an affidavit setting forth in detail the grounds or reasons why it is necessary to have more than one extradition agent, fugitive officer or person to be so designated. Among other things, and not by way of limitation, the affidavit shall set forth whether or not the alleged fugitive is a dangerous person, his previous criminal record if any, and any record of said fugitive on file with the Federal Bureau of Investigation or with the prison authorities of this State. As a further ground or reason for more than one extradition agent or fugitive officer to be designated, it may be shown in said affidavit the number of fugitives to be returned to this State and any other grounds or reasons for which more than one extradition agent or fugitive officer is desired. If the Governor finds or determines from his own investigation and from the information made available to him that more than one extradition agent or fugitive officer is necessary for the return of a fugitive or fugitives to this State, he may designate more than one extradition agent or fugitive officer for such purpose. All travel for which expenses or reimbursements are paid or allowed under this section shall be by the nearest, direct, convenient route of travel. If the extradition agent or agents or person or persons designated to return a fugitive or fugitives from another state to this State shall elect to travel by automobile, a sum not exceeding seven cents (7¢) per mile may be allowed in lieu of all travel expense, and which shall be paid upon a basis of mileage for the complete trip. The Governor may promulgate executive orders, rules and regulations governing travel, forms of statements, receipts or any other matter or objective provided for in this section. The Governor may delegate any or all of the duties, powers and responsibilities conferred upon him by this section to any executive agent or executive clerk on his staff or in his office, and such executive agent or executive clerk, when properly authorized, may perform any or all of the duties, powers and responsibilities conferred upon the Governor. Provided that if the fugitive from justice is an alleged felon, and he be returned without the service of extradition papers by the sheriff or the agent of the sheriff of the county in which the felony was alleged to have been committed, the expense of said return shall be borne by the State of North Carolina under the rules and regulations made and promulgated by the Governor of North Carolina or the executive agent or the executive clerk to whom the said Governor may have delegated his duties under this section. (1937, c. 273, s. 24; 1953, c. 1203; 1955, c. 289; 1973, c. 1286, s. 16; 1975, c. 166, s. 27; 1981, c. 859, s. 13.9.)

§ 15A–745. Immunity from service of process in certain civil actions.

A person brought into this State by, or after waiver of, extradition based on a criminal charge shall not be subject to service of personal process in civil actions arising out of the same facts as the criminal proceedings to answer which he is being or has been returned until he has been convicted in the criminal proceeding or, if acquitted, until he has had reasonable opportunity to return to the state from which he was extradited. (1937, c. 273, s. 25; 1973, c. 1286, s. 16.)

§ 15A–746. Written waiver of extradition proceedings.

Any person arrested in this State charged with having committed any crime in another state or alleged to have escaped from confinement, or broken the terms of his bail, probation or parole may waive the issuance and service of the warrant provided for in G.S. 15A-727 and 15A-728 and all other procedure incidental to extradition proceedings, by executing or subscribing in the presence of a judge of any court of record within this State or a clerk of the superior court a writing which states that he consents to return to the demanding state: Provided, however, that before such waiver shall be executed or subscribed by such person it shall be the duty of such judge or clerk of superior court to inform such person of his rights to the issuance and service of a warrant of extradition and to obtain a writ of habeas corpus as provided for in G.S. 15A-730.

If and when such consent has been duly executed it shall forthwith be forwarded to the office of the Governor of this State and filed therein. The judge or clerk of superior court shall direct the officer having such person in custody to deliver forthwith such person to the duly accredited agent or agents of the demanding state, and shall deliver or cause to be delivered to such agent or agents a copy of such consent: Provided, however, that nothing in this section shall be deemed to limit the rights of the accused person to return voluntarily and without formality to the demanding state, nor shall this waiver procedure be deemed to be an exclusive procedure or to limit the powers, rights or duties of the officers of the demanding state or of this State. (1937, c. 273, s. 25a; 1959, c. 271; 1973, c. 1286, s. 16.)

§ 15A–747. Nonwaiver by this State.

Nothing in this Article contained shall be deemed to constitute a waiver by this State of its right, power or privilege to try such demanded person for crime committed within this State, or of its right, power or privilege to regain custody of such person by extradition proceedings or otherwise for the purpose of trial, sentence or punishment for any crime committed within this State, nor shall any proceedings had under this Article which result in, or fail to result in, extradition be deemed a waiver by this State of any of its rights, privileges or jurisdiction in any way whatsoever. (1937, c. 273, s. 25b; 1973, c. 1286, s. 16.)

§ 15A–748. No right of asylum; no immunity from other criminal prosecution while in this State.

After a person has been brought back to this State by, or after waiver of, extradition proceedings, he may be tried in this State for other crimes which he may be charged with having committed here as well as that specified in the requisition for his extradition. (1937, c. 273, s. 26; 1973, c. 1286, s. 16.)

§ 15A–749. Interpretation.

The provisions of this Article shall be so interpreted and construed as to effectuate its general purposes to make uniform the law of those states which enact it. (1937, c. 273, s. 27; 1973, c. 1286, s. 16.)

§ 15A–750. Short title.

This Article may be cited as the Uniform Criminal Extradition Act. (1937, c. 273, s. 30; 1973, c. 1286, s. 16.)

Appendix

Agreement between Governor or District Attorney and the Armed Forces

_____
(date)

TO WHOM IT MAY CONCERN:

In consideration of the delivery of _____
(name of fugitive, grade, service number, and branch of armed forces)

_____ to _____ at _____, for trial
(county)   (city and state)

upon the charge of _____
(list charge or charges)

_____ ,

I hereby agree, pursuant to the authority vested in me as _____
(Governor or District Attorney)

_____, that the commanding officer in charge of the _____
(branch of service, location of

base or station, city and state)

and the Secretary of the _____ will be informed of the
(branch of service)

outcome of the trial and that said _____ will be returned to
(name of fugitive)

the _____ authorities at the place of delivery named above or to such
(name of branch of service)

other place as may be designated by the _____
(name of branch of service)

or issued transportation to the nearest receiving _____
(ship, station, or base)

without expense to the United States or to the person delivered, immediately upon the completion of the trial if the person is acquitted or immediately upon satisfying the sentence of the court if the person is convicted and a sentence imposed, or upon other disposition of the case, provided that the _____ authorities shall then desire his or her return.
(name of branch of service)

_____
(signature and typed name of Governor or District Attorney)

Return of Fugitive Notification Information and Reimbursement Request Form (page 1)

North Carolina Department of Public Safety
Extradition/ Fugitive Section

Pat McCrory, Governor
Kieran J. Shanahan, Secretary

Ssycret J. Evans, Section Chief

RETURN OF FUGITIVE NOTIFICATION INFORMATION AND REIMBURSEMENT REQUEST

THE EXTRADITION/FUGITIVE SECTION MUST APPROVE ALL REIMBURSEMENT REQUESTS PRIOR TO DISPATCH OF AGENT(S) FOR TRANSPORT OF THE FUGITIVE(S). ALL NECESSARY TRANSPORT AND SUBSISTENCE EXPENSES WILL BE REIMBURSED PURSUANT TO NORTH CAROLINA GENERAL STATUTE 15A-744. ALL TRANSPORTS MUST CONTAIN AN AGENT OF THE SAME SEX AS THE OFFENDER. THE INITIAL REQUEST SHALL BE MADE BY TELEPHONE TO THE EXTRADITION/FUGITIVE SECTION AT (919) 716-3190.

1. NAME AND ADDRESS OF AGENCY

2. NAME OF REQUESTING AGENT _____

3. LOCATION OF FUGITIVE _____
   (CITY AND STATE)

4. NAME OF FUGITIVE(S) _____

5. CHARGE(S)

6. DATE CALLED _____ DATE OF TRAVEL _____

7. MODE OF TRAVEL: ( ) CAR ( ) AIR

8.

9. FUGITIVE STATUS: ( ) WAIVED ( ) GOVERNOR'S WARRANT
   ( ) INTERSTATE AGREEMENT ON DETAINERS

10. APPROVED BY: _____

11. TRANSPORTING AGENT(S) ASSIGNED:

Page 1 of 2

MAILING ADDRESS:
4224 Mail Service Center
Raleigh, NC 27699-4224
Telephone: (919) 716-3190

OFFICE LOCATION:
2020 Yonkers Road
Raleigh, NC 27604
Fax: (919) 716-3991
ORI: NC092065G

www.ncdps.gov
An Equal Opportunity employer

Return of Fugitive Notification Information and Reimbursement Request Form (page 2)

LOCAL LAW ENFORCEMENT AGENCY REIMBURSEMENT REQUEST FOR RETURN OF FUGITIVE

INSTRUCTIONS: This form is to be used by Local Government Law Enforcement Agencies ONLY. Use this form whenever transporting a fugitive(s), include ALL expenses and attach all necessary expense receipt(s). If you have questions concerning this form, please telephone the Extradition/Fugitive Section at (919) 716-3190.

This is to certify that the expenses listed below are true and accurate and were necessary in returning:

_____

Name of Fugitive(s)

to_____

City and County

North Carolina to stand trial on the felony charge(s) of

_____

_____

1. Dates of Travel: Date Departed_____ Date Returned_____
2. Time of Day Departed_____ Time Returned_____
3. SUBSTANCE AND TRAVEL COST ESTIMATES:

    A. MEALS:

        No. of Breakfast _____ x $ 8.00 x No. of Officers _____ = $_____

        No. of Lunches _____ x $ 10.45 x No. of Officers _____ = $_____

        No. of Dinner
        (In-State) _____ x $ 17.90 x No. of Officers _____ = $_____
        (Out of State) _____ x $ 20.30 x No. of Officers _____ = $_____

    B. LODGING:
        No. of Nights_____ x _____ x No. of Officers _____ = $_____
        (Receipt must be attached)

        TRAVEL:
        Automobile trip to _____
        (Location)
        Total Miles Driven _____ x .30 =$_____

        Air Travel Actual Costs (attach receipt) =$_____

    C. OTHER EXPENSES: **(Include all receipts and explain cost)** =$_____

    D. TOTAL AMOUNT DUE (City/County) =$_____

_____Sheriff/Police Chief

(Signature)

This is to certify that the above named fugitive was returned to North Carolina on the felony charge as shown above.

_____ District Attorney

(Signature)

NAME AND ADDRESS OF AGENCY

_____

_____

_____

INTERNAL USE ONLY		
		Amount
Budget Code	14550	_____
Fund	1394	_____
Total amount to be reimbursed		_____

Page 2 of 2

www.ingramcontent.com/pod-product-compliance
Lightning Source LLC
Chambersburg PA
CBHW061838220326
41599CB00027B/5323